On Wings of Spirit

"Whatsoever things are true, whatsoever things are honest, whatsoever thinge are just, whatsoever things are pure, whatsoever things are lovely, whatsoever things are of good report . . . think on these things."

St. Paul. Phil. 3:20/21.

"A study of the past reveals the future."

Teilhard de Chardin.

"Read not to contradict and confute, nor to believe and take for granted, but to weigh and consider . . . Histories make men wise."

Francis Bacon.

ON WINGS OF SPIRIT

Percy E. Corbett

*

an autobiography

THE RESEARCH PUBLISHING CO.
52 Lincoln's Inn Fields · London

Also by Percy Corbett

THE ETERNAL STAIRWAY
THE POWER OF THE SPIRIT
WHY BRITAIN?
MAKING CHURCH HISTORY

ISBN 0 7050 0044 3
Printed in Great Britain for The Research Publishing Co.
(Fudge & Co. Ltd.), London

CONTENTS

ACKNOWLEDGMENTS

I gratefully acknowledge permission from the following to use material from their letters or publications:

The Churches' Fellowship for Psychical and Spiritual Studies.

Miss Grace Rosher.

Psychic Press Ltd.

The Mitre Press.

Mrs. Helen Greaves.

The Rev'd. Leonard Argyle.

Dr. Robert Crookall.

Mrs. C. J. Toyne.

Helios Book Service Ltd.

The College of Psychic Studies.

Miss I. Wigram.

PREFACE

It gives me real pleasure to recommend this book to a wide range of readers.

Percy Corbett claims to be no scholar. He writes not as an intellectual, but as an ordinary man in the street for other men and women in the street. They are numerous. Like him they did not enjoy, or endure, formal education into their late teens or early twenties but went to work much sooner on humdrum jobs. Many of them may find that they feel much as he does about the life we lead.

The book is largely autobiographical, the personal story of one man's quest for the truth. Much use is made of quotations from other men's work, yet the selection chosen is so personal as almost to add to the sense of autobiography. Many of the statements, perhaps even most of the book, may well be found controversial, but even so the story unfolded is bound to stir chords of memory and of shared experience in the minds and hearts of many. It is not only the author of this book but many others besides who can detect in the daily events and apparent coincidences of this life, patterns that reveal the presence of underlying forces. To such discerning travellers through the spiritual wilderness of this world the book offers the benediction, if I may translate it into the words of James Elroy Flecker:—

> "God be thy guide from camp to camp: God be thy shade from well to well:
> God grant beneath the desert stars thou hear the Prophet's camel bell.
> And God shall make thy body pure, and give thee knowledge to endure
> This ghost-life's piercing phantom-pain and bring thee out to Life again."

In this material age any man does a service to his fellows who even for a short time can raise the level of thought and aspiration above the material and cause us to concentrate our attention on higher and more permanent values. It is astonishing that man succeeds in so enclosing himself within his own culture that he can, and does in practice, disregard such important issues, with such a close relevance to the aims and conduct of life on this Earth, as the nature of life after death; or that the vast and obvious extent of things we still do not know does not shake the complacency of belief in the total explicability of the world in terms of human science or politics or religion. In the last few years there has been a rather sudden awakening to the importance of looking after our planet lest we should destroy its capacity for going on looking after us. This is encouraging. If such a thing can happen it may also be that before too long the spiritual light may be able to break through more widely into human hearts and minds to lift our aspirations and infuse a more worthwhile purpose into our lives, one with so broad an appeal as to be recognisable and acceptable to all races of men, bringing them at last to a sense of unity that has not yet been achieved. If Percy Corbett's book can contribute even a little to such a development a life's effort will have been more than worthwhile.

Lake House, G. B. Blaker.
Ockley, Surrey. 8th June 1976.

PART I

I

BOYHOOD STIRRINGS

As this book will relate patterns in my life, both as an individual and also in association with other people, it seems essential that I should begin with some of my early memories and background.

I was born on the 29th May 1908 in Craven Arms, a small town in South Shropshire. I was greatly privileged in having the benefit of parents with good and lasting qualities who expressed something of benefit to others by the way they lived.

My father worked for a local firm of auctioneers and the nature of his work brought him in touch with country people over a large area. He was kind, gentle, cheerful, hard-working and very popular wherever he went. He never sought material possessions or personal gain and he was the first local married man to volunteer for military service in 1914. He had no strong link with organised religion.

My mother was the daughter of a farmer. She was not only a devout Christian but practised Christian teachings in her daily life. She combined gentleness with a strength of character and a will-power which continuously drove her physical powers beyond their reasonable limits.

An example of my mother's outlook is contained in the following prayer which was among other verses which she had copied out and retained for reference:

A Woman's Prayer

O Lord, who knowest every need of mine,
Help me to bear each cross and not repine.
Grant me fresh courage every day,
Help me to do my work alway
Without complaint.

O Lord, Thou knowest well how dark the way,
Guide Thou my footsteps lest they stray,
Give me fresh faith for every hour,
Lest I should ever doubt Thy power
And make complaint.

Give me a heart, O Lord, strong to endure,
Help me to keep it simple, pure,
Make me unselfish, helpful, true,
In every act, whate'er I do
And keep content.

In many ways, she had a hard life. During my father's absence from 1914 to 1918, she brought up three children, dug and planted the garden, encouraged us to qualify for secondary education and to learn the piano and also took in dressmaking as well as making many of our clothes.

My link with my mother was a strong one and, after I left home, we both maintained the link by a weekly letter without any difficulty.

With these qualities of character in my parents, although we were not well off, our home was a happy one and I have pleasant memories of evenings spent playing cards at home, either among ourselves or with friends. Also of songs or hymns, especially with Welsh relatives, around the piano. They were simple pleasures but we were expressing ourselves naturally and they seemed much more satisfying than passing hours watching programmes on television as many people do today.

I remember taking pots of jam, rice puddings and other items of food to visiting young men of the Church Army. My mother also helped them by doing their washing and inviting them home for meals and a chat.

Our parish church was at Stokesay, a mile and a quarter away, where the 12th century church with oak pews adjoined Stokesay Castle. It nestles in a valley surrounded by small hills. In those days, most of the hills were covered by trees and it was very pleasant walking to church on a Sunday morning in the Autumn with the changing colours of the leaves and the beautiful sound of the church bells pealing across the countryside,

This part of South Shropshire is essentially an agricultural area and I well remember the horse sales when about 400 horses would be sold at one sale. Also, the sheep sales when the mornings would be filled with the variable baa-ing notes of the sheep, each flock gaily coloured with sheep dye, as they were driven along the various country roads to the sale. They had to walk many miles to the sales in those days and there were sometimes up to 20,000 ewes at one sale. This was said to be the largest ewe sale in the country.

The licensee of the Stokesay Hotel used to make cider from apples in his orchard every year. He hired cider presses in which the apples were squeezed through hessian and the juice collected. It was a manual operation and we boys were given a shilling each for giving a helping hand.

In the summer, my father assisted with the harvesting of hay on the auctioneer's farm and I have happy memories of accompanying my mother carrying tea to the fields and having picnics with the delightful smell of new-mown hay. The hay was taken to the farm on large horse-drawn wagons which were also used for Sunday School 'treats'.

When I was nine years old, I had an operation for the removal of tonsils and, following this experience, I contracted asthma which affected my life considerably. For many years, the attacks were variable but generally severe. They would usually commence in the early hours of the morning and would result in the loss of many hours sleep with the consequent feeling of lethargy during the following day. In those days, it was not possible to obtain quick relief by using drugs and it was a case of 'grinning and bearing' it.

Naturally, this limited my activities as I was always short of breath. It also severely affected my education. After gaining a place in the King Edward II Grammar School at Ludlow and starting well by winning a form prize, asthma intervened and the rest of my schooldays were a constant struggle.

It was during one of my spells at home that our local vicar called. When chatting with me, he asked me whether I had ever thought of entering the church. He was a saintly old man and I have wondered since whether he sensed the missionary potential which was to develop at a later stage in my life.

One of my boyhood friends worked for a local newsagent and it was because of knowing him that I first read a magazine called

Health and Strength. This magazine contained a number of articles about weak men who became strong by taking up physical culture. Having spent many lonely hours during the night fighting for breath, passing away the time by reading, etc., I reacted strongly to the possibility of getting personal benefit through physical culture and commenced carrying out daily exercises, walking, deep breathing, etc. I became stronger, gained weight and, later on, found myself unexpectedly organising local youths in a gymnasium in a neighbouring village. At one time, this was attended by 60 youths, one of whom cycled 12 miles in all types of weather to attend the sessions.

About this period, I remember, when walking with a friend on a sunny Sunday afternoon, spontaneously reacting to the joy of Nature at its best by doffing my trilby hat and saying, "I take my hat off to it!" Was this a sense of an atunement with God through Nature?

When I was confirmed at Stokesay Church by the Bishop of Hereford, I clearly remember something "leap" inside me. Was it imagination or spiritual experience?

In my youth, I was always an idealist and, in a groping way, I tried to be a practical idealist. The motto of the Health and Strength League was "Sacred thy Body even as thy Soul". I joined the League and was a member for many years.

I also joined the Paladins' League which was a group based on the knights of old formed by Lt. Col. G. S. Hutchinson, DSO, MC, author of *The W. Plan*, etc.

The badge of the Paladins took the form of a clenched fist with the words "WE WILL' which were an abbreviation of the motto:

"WE WILL make this a better world both for ourselves and our Sons and Daughters, and WE WILL lay the foundations for a still better world — mentally, physically and morally". Lt. Col. Hutchinson was a "Baden Powell' type of man whose fascinating life story is told in his biography *Footslogger* by Graham Seton.

Naturally, the Boy Scout Movement attracted me but there was no local troop at the time I was the right age. However, a troop was formed later on and I became associated with it becoming Assistant Scoutmaster, Rover Scout Leader and I also helped with the Wolf Cub Pack.

I had ideas of becoming a chemist when leaving school in 1924 but the examinations were beyond my capacity so, after working in the office of a local garage for a few months, I started work at the local Post Office. I was pleased that my training included learning morse for the transmission of telegrams.

My hours of duty varied with the result that, on sunny mornings in the summer, I was able to cycle to the nearby Longmynd range of hills. After ascending to a reasonable height, I would strip off my clothes and lie on my cycling cape in the morning sun for a few hours. (Was this another intuitive reaching out to God through Nature?). These were very pleasant interludes with just the usual country sounds and the stirring songs of skylarks and plaintive calls of curlews.

II

REACHING OUT

By 1931, I felt that I needed more experience in my daily work and, after making enquiries at Post Offices in Leamington Spa, Warwick, Cheltenham, Gloucester, Oxford and Banbury, I found that there was a vacancy at Banbury in Oxfordshire. As Banbury was situated on a main railway line which would simplify visits home, and the hours of duties were much more reasonable than those in the other Post Offices, I decided to transfer there and made the change in September.

Although I did not maintain my link with the church, my idealism was expressed by linking up with the Rover Scouts and by reviving a local Health and Strength Club, becoming a League District Officer of the Health and Strength League in order to do so.

In addition, I joined the local Rambling Club and became its secretary for four years. Walking around the countryside of Oxfordshire, Warwickshire and Northamptonshire gave me great enjoyment. I well remember expressing this enjoyment by saying, "I shall be doing this all my life!" Needless to say, although this statement was expressed with all sincerity at the time, other commitments prevented me from carrying out this intention.

During this period, I became interested in politics and attended a few weekend schools arranged by the Workers' Educational Association. While I was studying politics, I became aware of a strange apathy among the majority of people. I found that most people were not concerned with the current problems of life. For instance, the Old Age Pension at that time was 10 shillings per week and anyone who really investigated this recognised that it was insufficient to provide a pensioner living by himself with reasonable means of existence — especially during the winter. But I found that most people were not concerned about this human problem which was so obvious to me. I found, too, that whilst my mother appreciated the problem and agreed that something should be done about it, she was unaware that her local M.P. had voted against a proposed increase in the amount of the Old Age Pension.

This problem of apathy concerning what, to me, were vital problems of life appeared insoluble until something occurred which 'triggered off' a very important pattern in my thinking and, therefore, in my life. We describe certain happenings loosely as 'Fate', 'Coincidences', 'Strokes of Luck' and so on but is there not a logical explanation why there should be an important effect in lives as a result of two strangers meeting for the first time? I believe now that such meetings are arranged by benevolent beings in the spirit world who are interested in our welfare and our need for spiritual expansion and that they arrange such meetings by telepathic impressions into the minds of the people concerned.

What happened to me did not seem significant at the time. I merely met a member of the staff at Banbury Post Office who was a Theosophist and who loaned me some books on Theosophy. The word "Theosophy" means "Divine Wisdom" and I found that Theosophists claimed to have an inner wisdom about life and its purpose. They teach that life is constantly evolving from a lower to a higher state and that this growth of consciousness can be seen in Nature. We know, of course, of the movement within the atomic structure of minerals. Theosophists teach that there is a low form of life in the mineral world and that it is then expressed in a higher form in the vegetable world. Anyone who thinks about the growth and beauty of trees and flowers must agree that there is a higher form of expression. There is much more movement as in climbing plants, there is a higher degree of consciousness as in the tropical plant which catches flies and the extent of the addition of beauty in flowers and the foliage of shrubs and trees is obvious.

Next we come to the animal kingdom. Animals have freedom of movement. They are not rooted to one spot like most flowers, shrubs and trees. They show signs of intelligence and, when domesticated and shown friendship and love by man, they respond with attributes like faithfulness, friendship, obedience and so on. Although I have read of people who claim to commune with trees, one does not normally find these attributes in the vegetable world.

After the animal kingdom comes man. Here one's mind boggles with thoughts of the finding of remains of early man — half a million years old — with the tremendous range of intelligence and character expressed by individual members of the human race. From the idiot to the genius and from the criminal to the saint. Theosophists teach that man is taking part in an upward path of evolution, that he reincarnates in physical bodies to undergo experiences which are only available in earthly lives and that he then continues to evolve on spiritual planes.

I could only accept the Theosophist teaching as a theory but I found it intensely interesting as I began to apply it to some of the problems in life with which I was concerned. If this teaching were true, it explained the apathy which I had found in relation to Old Age Pensions. It seemed to me that the basic theme of character in the evolution of man was a degree of selfishness or unselfishness. Extreme selfishness in the case of the hardened criminal and remarkable unselfishness in the saintly type of man; the average man being a variable mixture of both. Thus the person who was generally more selfish than unselfish would not be concerned with the well-being of other people, whether they were Old Age Pensioners or other classes of the community.

I could only treat this teaching as a theory but I felt that, if it were true, it was of the utmost importance and that, whenever possible, I must put it to the test. This period was an important one as it proved to be the turning point in my life when I seriously sought deeper truths concerning the purpose and meaning of life. As it can be traced to meeting one person and the opening up of new realms of knowledge, I wonder how often this type of experience happens to other people, to what degree we can create such opportunities by always maintaining an open mind or to what degree we block these patterns by maintaining a closed mind and thinking that our learning stopped when we left school?

III

SOME EXPERIENCES DURING MILITARY SERVICE

On the strength of my knowledge of Morse Code, I joined the Supplementary Reserve of the Royal Corps of Signals in 1932. As I married in 1934, I found the reservist pay of especial benefit. It meant, however, that I was immediately called up on the outbreak of war in September 1939. This commenced another pattern in my life which lasted for six years.

My call-up for military service coincided with the time when I had decided to try and test the teachings of Theosophy. I reported for army service at Catterick Camp in Yorkshire and, because I was posted to an Officer Cadet Training Unit, remained there for over three years. As soon as I had become settled in my new situation, I began to use my spare time to continue my quest.

One of the problems facing me was that of the continuity of life and individual survival after death. From a common-sense point of view, assuming the theory of consciousness expanding through the mineral, vegetable and animal worlds to man, it seemed logical that this continuous expansion should continue beyond a short earthly life and not stop at man. I heard a contemporary and respected scientist, Sir Oliver Lodge, state on the radio his personal conviction of individual survival after death.

He ended his broadcast with the following words:

> The veil between the two worlds is wearing thin. It is possible, given the right conditions, to communicate with those we call dead. They are still mindful of our love for them and they reciprocate it fully. They are hurt by our excessive grief at their loss. They do not think of themselves as dead, but as now fully alive, free of the clogging body and

able to move freely in their new state, using the etheric body which they possessed all the time.

I did not arrive at this belief by a religious channel. It was based on the facts and experiences studied in the large and comprehensive science which, in my view, should take into account the whole of the phenomena, not limit itself to material phenomena . . . It is this larger science that I humbly and unworthily try to represent. It removes all fear of the unknown and encourages trust — trust in God as a loving Father.

The fact that a scientist could broadcast such conviction to the world encouraged me to investigate Spiritualism. I knew nothing about the subject and approached it with the idea that I would always use my reason in my search for truth and would not accept other peoples' beliefs in this subject. I thought that the followers of Spiritualism were generally elderly ladies and I felt that my reason, which I regarded as a gift of God which could be applied to any subject, would lead me to the truth.

On making local enquiries, I found that Spiritualist meetings were held at Darlington, a town 14 miles from Catterick Camp, and I began attending them from time to time. At the same time, I was reading books on Spiritualism and allied subjects and, later on, I read a weekly psychic newspaper regularly.

At first, I was disappointed with the general standard at the Spiritualist services as compared with the wonderful happenings I had read in books. Gradually, however, I began to absorb what one might call "grains of truth". I felt that I must search for truth and that the saying, "There is nothing higher than Truth" was very important. I found, too, that from time to time, I would react in such a way that I would have an inner feeling that something I heard, read or experienced was true. It now appears that I was using an intuitive faculty which is common to all men and is described in the following passage in *Mysticism* [1] by F. C. Happold:

"Though it may be to a great extent atrophied and exist only potentially in most men, men possess an organ or faculty which is capable of discerning spiritual truth and, in its own spheres, this faculty is as much to be relied on as are other organs of sensation in theirs".

[1] Penguin Books

During my visits to the Spiritualist services at Darlington, I received various "messages" from mediums which proved to be a mixture of items recognised, items not recognised and items prophesied for the future — some of which happened as forecast. (It seems evident that a medium is a highly sensitive "receiver" and "transmitter" and that much of the material transmitted is subject to the interpretation of symbolic mental impression). These included my brother John — one message correctly specifying consumption as the cause of his death, my maternal grandmother and a schoolboy friend who died while I was at school. His surname of "Wakefield" was correctly given.

A description of a relative was given by a child spirit guide as, "A lady who wore old-fashioned clothes, a blouse with buttons down the front, long skirts and elastic-sided boots. She used to push her glasses up on her forehead, forget where they were and then look around for them. A roundish face with a high forehead, grey hair taken back." This was a very good description of my father's cousin, Lucy Corfield.

Several mediums spoke of a little girl with me whom I did not recognize but I confirmed that she could have been a sister lost in pregnancy. Descriptions were:

(1) *28th March 1942.* A medium, name not recorded, said that she "saw" a beautiful fair-haired little girl who would be my guide.

(2) *20th June 1942.* A spirit guide described a little girl with fair hair. Large bow and ringlets, blue eyes, long eyelashes and a round face. She had been stillborn when I was a small boy. She would act as a guide to me with impressions of simplicity.

(3) *15th July 1942.* Mrs. E. Smith of Darlington described a beautiful little girl with a round face, fair hair and blue eyes who was probably a stillborn sister.

In May 1942, I visited a professional medium in Darlington. His comment was that I had missed my vocation. I should have been either a clergyman, a chemist or a doctor. In view of my spare-time missionary work, the fact that I considered becoming a chemist and that I am interested in people with mental troubles and am co-operating with local Health Visitors, this was an interesting remark.

As time went on, I met other soldiers who were interested in Spiritualism and we formed a small group in our unit. I also received a gift of twenty books on psychic matters and, eventually, built up a library. A man joined our unit who had been a medium for many years and I was delighted to have this opportunity of studying a medium at close quarters. He was a man of undoubted sincerity and integrity with a cheerful personality. We used to meet regularly in the Toc H. Room at Richmond, a small town four miles from Catterick Camp.

One Sunday, our group officiated at the evening service at a Spiritualist Church at Darlington. We were announced on their Notice Board outside the church as "Our Soldier Friends from Catterick". The church was packed to capacity. Our medium friend gave the address and demonstration, one young man led the prayers, one sang a solo, I played the organ for the hymns and the rest of the group supported us by their presence. This combined effort was very successful and the following letter was received at a later date:

Dear Friends,

Regardless of formality and not perhaps ever being given the privilege of congratulating you, I feel greatly impressed to write you these few lines in appreciation of a most beautiful service that you and your inspirers rendered to your God and fellowmen last Sunday evening, the 29th November 1942. Also, in sincere admiration for the divine way in which you all worked so harmoniously.

I pray that God's Blessing may rest upon each one of you and that you may be given the opportunity in every pathway of this life that you may tread to carry your torch of light so high and so gloriously bright that it may illuminate and enlighten everyone with whom you come into contact.

In conclusion, I beg your pardon for what may seem to be an audacity, but is in all sincerity a thought actuated with the best intentions.

Yours faithfully,

A Friendly Observer.

In addition to gaining experiences in the Spiritualist field, I carried out experiments in telepathy with a young Scot who was an M.A. We obtained a sufficient proportion of partially correct results to arouse our curiosity but our experiments had to stop when my friend was transferred to another unit. We corresponded from time to time and I received a letter from him when I was in Italy in March 1945. When commenting on our association at Catterick Camp, he wrote, "It was the happiest and most spiritually contented time I have ever known."

Another member of the group called unexpectedly to see me in 1951 when I was working at the Atomic Energy Establishment at Aldermaston in Berkshire. He obtained work there, moved with his family from Southampton and, at the time of writing this book, is helping to organise meetings for the discussion and furtherance of spiritual truths in the Aldermaston area.

At one period, I was in charge of the Cadet Wing Office and, on checking the records of the cadets' religious persuasions to find out whether there were any Spiritualists among the total of 500, I found that one had recorded his religion as "Spiritualist". I contacted him and we had a few interesting chats. His mother was a medium and he very kindly arranged for her to send me some books, one of which recorded her personal experiences. These experiences were deeply spiritual in their nature and I was very impressed by them.

Like other cadets, he completed his training and then left the training unit. Apart from a few letters, we lost touch with each other. It is interesting, however, that, in March 1942, he wrote a letter to me which included these words, "I feel that we shall meet again; probably because each of us is going in the same direction." His forecast came true 22 years later when we met unexpectedly at a Spiritual and Cultural Interlude at "Roselaleham" in Devon in July 1964.

In February 1943, I was transferred to a unit in London and this gave me opportunities to gain further experience by visiting seances and hearing mediums of a higher standard. Within 24 hours of my arrival in London, I believe that there was evidence of spirit guidance. I arrived in North London late one Friday evening. The following afternoon I went for a walk in order to familiarise myself with my new surroundings. On reaching the nearest main road and a few shops, I went into a newsagent's shop and enquired if he could obtain the weekly newspaper *Psychic News* for me. He was doubtful in view of the war-time conditions. I also asked him if he knew the address of the local

Spiritualist church. He replied that he thought that there was a Spiritualist church at Golders Green but, if I asked the lady in the shop on the opposite side of the road, she could probably give me more details. I went to the other shop as directed and repeated my enquiry to an elderly lady with a majestic air. She asked me why I wanted the information. When I told her that I was very interested in Spiritualism, she asked if I could return at seven o'clock when the shop would be closed and it would be easier to talk. I agreed to do this and duly returned in the evening. She asked me further questions and then told me that she had a friend who was a true psychic, her emphasis on the word "true" implying that her friend had higher gifts than the average Spiritualist medium. She also said that she and her friend held monthly meetings in her flat over the shop and that, if I was interested, she would ask her friend if I could attend her meetings. I asked how her friend would decide this without meeting me. She replied that her friend was a *true* psychic and that she would know.

A week later, the lady at the shop confirmed that I could attend their meetings. I found both ladies very intelligent and reasonable. They both believed in reincarnation, that the British are God's Chosen People, that they were both descendants of Gad (Gen. 30: 11). The meetings usually took the form of long talks given through the trance mediumship of the psychic lady.

Two other experiences stand out in my memory. One was a public meeting at which Leslie Flint was the medium. His mediumship took the form known as Independent Voice. He sat in a "cabinet" which was rather like a sentry-box on the stage with some of his close friends on either side. A microphone was placed on the front of the stage several yards in front of the "cabinet". Voices, which were alleged to be spirit voices, spoke to the audience of about 200 over the loud-speaker equipment. Many were recognised and one speaker was said to be the well-known author, Conan Doyle. Electrical engineers, with no interest in Spiritualism, testified that no-one sitting in the "cabinet" could be heard speaking over the loud-speaker equipment. After the war, I attended several seances with Leslie Flint with a small group. Tape recordings were made on these occasions and I am satisfied that his mediumship was genuine.

The other experience was that of Direct Voice mediumship when I attended a seance with about 20 other people. This was my first experience of physical mediumship of this kind. Voices spoke through trumpets to those present and conversations took place. In addition, two trumpets gyrated in the air at such a speed and with such accuracy that it seemed impossible that they were controlled by a human agency.

During my stay in London, I discovered that a Corporal in the Orderly Room was interested in Spiritualism and had carried out communication with the spirit world by the use of an upturned tumbler which was placed on a smooth surface in the centre of a circle formed by letters of the alphabet and the words "Yes" and "No". When fingers were placed on the bottom of the tumbler it moved to various letters and these made up words.

I was naturally interested in gaining practical experience and this was quite new to me. We tried it on many occasions and found that it worked and that the messages received were reasonable.

On one occasion, the Corporal was told in this manner to visit his brother, who lived just outside London, before the weekend. He queried why he should go before the weekend and was told that his brother, who had been estranged from his family, was visiting Manchester, where their mother lived, at the weekend. The spirit communicator wanted the Corporal to ask his brother to visit their mother and patch up the family quarrel.

As we were busy in the Orderly Room at that time, the Corporal and I discussed the possibility of the visit and, after referring to railway time-tables, he agreed to go. I lost touch with the Corporal until we met again in Southern Italy in 1944. He was able to show me a letter from his mother in which she wrote how pleased she was that the other brother had returned to the family circle. Having been present when the message was received which 'triggered off' this pattern which proved helpful, I found this sequel very interesting indeed as it confirmed the Spiritualist belief in spirit guidance.

In May 1943, our unit embarked at Liverpool for overseas duty from which I did not return until September 1945. We disembarked at Algiers and I spent a few months in North Africa, a few months in Sicily and nearly two years in Italy.

During this period, I was receiving the weekly psychic newspaper and, for much of the time, a monthly book from the Psychic Book Club. I was also discussing the subject with anyone whom I found to be interested. One man with whom I discussed the evolutionary theory was a B.Sc. and he agreed with the theory so far as his studies in biology were concerned but, like most people, he was not interested in its application to man. This, to me, was the most vital part of the problem and I was amazed, and am still amazed (21 years later) at the general ignorance and lack of interest in this deeper aspect of life.

In July 1943, in sending details of my meeting with a girl serving in the A.T.S. whose parents were mediums, I wrote to my wife, "I am sending the Airgraph to show how I want to meet people, irrespective of sex and, by my beliefs and personality, pull them up to higher things. This is a good example because I hardly knew this girl. I only met her once and yet the phrases she uses are expressive of good results in so short a time and it gives me confidence that I am developing along the right lines and generally gaining sufficient knowledge of the real truth of life to help other people which is what I want to do."

In the same letter I wrote, "I've had several chats on philosophy with Sergeant Howard and gave him four typewritten sheets on life as I saw it. The odd thing was that, later on, when discussing the necessary qualities for those in power, he turned up a book and quoted sayings by Plato over 2000 years ago. They were practically word for word the same as the views I had typed and given him. This means that Truth does not alter through the centuries."

In April 1944, we had left North Africa and, after staying some months in Sicily, we were stationed in a small village about 12 miles from Bari in Southern Italy. A Despatch Rider Section, composed mainly of young men, was attached to the headquarters of our Air Formation Unit. At that time, this Section was holding a weekly meeting for the discussion of any subject of topical interest. Knowing of my practical interest, the sergeant in charge of the young Despatch Riders invited me to speak to them on Spiritualism. Although I was well aware of the limitations of my knowledge, I agreed to do this. The meeting was successful and many questions were asked. In addition, I was asked if I could give them some proof of survival after death.

I replied that I was not a medium but, if they nominated a representative to hold a separate meeting with their sergeant and myself, I would try and obtain some evidence for their consideration. They nominated one of the older members of the Section who was an insurance agent and he, the sergeant and I tried the inverted tumbler and alphabet method of communication which had proved successful in London. The tumbler moved and the name "John Haigh" was spelled out. I questioned the spelling of "Haigh" as I had not seen the word spelled with the letter "h" at the end. The spelling was confirmed and I questioned the others. The sergeant did not know the name but the insurance agent recognised it. Three names were then spelled out which the insurance agent said were those of John Haigh's wife and daughter and his own daughter who went to school with John Haigh's daughter. He told us that John Haigh was a friend of his who had died as a result of burns received in a military camp.

About 10 years later, I was relating this experience to members of a Discussion Group at a Spiritualist Church at Oxford when, much to my surprise, one of the members confirmed the details of John Haigh's death, saying that she knew the family at the time of the fire in the camp.

As the Allies advanced up Italy, we moved further north and stayed some months at a small town called Vasto which was situated on the Adriatic coast. The army had set up a department which was known as A.B.C.A. (The Army Bureau for Current Affairs) and literature was distributed so that officers could keep the men up-to-date on national and international matters. In February 1945, our Assistant Adjutant, who was responsible for the local A.B.C.A. lectures, told me that he could not find a suitable subject for the current week's lecture. I offered to give a talk on Evolution and Psychic Experiences. He agreed and the talk was very successful. At the end of the talk, the Assistant Adjutant invited suggestions for the following week's lecture and he was asked if I could speak again. He agreed to this and the second talk was also very successful.

While we were at Vasto, I made enquiries concerning psychic matters among the local Italians and, as a result, I was able to meet a retired chemist who had been a member of the Italian Society of Metaphysics. He told me that he had been used for automatic writing when he was younger. As I hoped to visit Rome, he gave me a letter of introduction to the President of the Society. When I went to Rome for six days leave, I visited the President but he was ill and he gave me the address of the secretary, Professor Clepis. Professor Clepis made me very welcome and told me that they had 500 members of the Society, many of them being doctors. He had a card index of mediums in various parts of the world and showed me correspondence with societies in Britain and America. He had a combination lock in his possession which had belonged to his father. His father had died without telling his family details of the combination and it remained locked for 40 years until a medium in Rome gave Professor Clepis the secret and he was able to open the lock. I visited this medium who said that she had permission from the Roman Catholic Church to carry out experiments for the Society of Metaphysics. I also visited another medium and a report of my visit was printed on the front page of *Psychic News* dated 28th April 1945, under the heading "British Soldier finds Mediums in Rome. Fascism and the Vatican could not stop them."

During our stay at Vasto, I attended classes in the Italian language. The teacher was an Austrian lady who told me that she knew that she was psychic but she could not see any advantage in developing her gifts. I loaned her several Spiritualist books which reported the experiences of well-known British mediums.

It was also whilst we were in Vasto in April 1945 that I received a letter from the Reverend Frost, a Church of England minister with whom I had been corresponding and to whom I had sent long extracts from the philosophy given by a well-known spirit guide in Hannen Swaffer's Home Circle in London.

In one letter he wrote, "I do agree with all that is said in this most interesting exposition. I have read it most carefully and truthfully do agree with it all." In relating this extract to my wife I wrote, "He is a clever, good man so that's just one more sign that I'm working on the right lines."

I was released from Army service in September 1945 with a feeling that my reading experiences in my quest for truth had been invaluable but that I needed more practical experience.

IV

SPIRITUALISM

As I had been promoted *in absentia* to a clerical grade I was transferred from the Post Office at Banbury and commenced work at Oxford in December 1945, eventually moving to live in Oxford in 1947.

Shortly after returning to civilian life, I read an advertisement from someone in Banbury who wished to form a Spiritualist Home Circle. Home Circles are described as the 'Backbone of Spiritualism' and they are formed by a small intimate group who meet once a week for the purpose of psychic development and spirit communication. The leader then says an extempore prayer and members sit quietly endeavouring to still the normal conscious activity of the mind so that a calm and receptive mental state is reached. This is the mental condition which permits psychic gifts to unfold.

When there is perfect harmony and sincerity among the group forming a Home Circle, a spiritual atmosphere is created. This atmosphere may be similar to that created by the early Christians who followed the teaching of Jesus recorded in St. Matthew 18:20, "For where two or three are gathered together in my name, there am I in the midst of them."

I have heard a member of a Home Circle describing her reaction as "like going to church". I also remember enquiring how a lady felt after her first visit to a Home Circle and her reply that she had never felt so relaxed in all her life.

I joined the Home Circle which was being formed at Banbury and this gave me the opportunity of meeting other enquirers and to witness the gradual development of mediumship.

For two years I chatted with fellow travellers during my journeys to and from Oxford. One of them borrowed books on Spiritualism and I found out later that this man's cousin was reading the books with growing interest. Eventually, I met the cousin and formed a link with him which resulted in his joining the Home Circle at Banbury.

After moving to Oxford I joined the local Spiritualist Church and this action commenced another pattern of valuable experience. As I was the secretary of this church for several years, I met many mediums, ran a Discussion Group for two years, organised public meetings and met leading officials in the Spiritualists' National Union.

I felt strongly that there were wonderful truths in Spiritualism which were not expressed in orthodox religion, that the knowledge and proof of survival after death could remove fears, give people a stronger faith in God and bring peace to the world. Working within the Spiritualist movement, I knew how much people were being helped by the Spiritualist teachings and demonstrations of mediumship. I was aware that the national press avoided reports of these activities unless a case of a fake medium came to notice. Knowing of the way in which many ordinary men and women were sincerely using their gifts for the benefit of humanity, I felt that this was unfair and that valuable knowledge was being withheld from the public.

A man came to the Spiritualist Church who had suffered from a large duodenal ulcer which had been confirmed by an X-ray photograph. He told me that he had had a psychic operation which was carried out through the trance mediumship of Mr. J. J. Thomas. He had informed his doctor what had occurred and the doctor arranged a further X-ray. This showed that the duodenal ulcer had been removed, apparently by a surgical operation, although no incision had been made in the patient's skin.

As a result of this experience, I organised a public meeting in the hall of the Oxford branch of the St. John Ambulance Brigade at which Mr. J. J. Thomas demonstrated his psychic healing operations. Despite bad weather, it was a very successful meeting. It aroused local interest and created a controversy in the correspondence columns of the local newspapers.

We did not wish to make any financial gain from this meeting and the profits were offered to the local branch of the St. John Ambulance Brigade. By this time, the head of their county organisation was concerned that their hall had been used for such a purpose. He was a doctor and his criticism resulted in their refusal to accept the proceeds from the meeting. The amount was then offered to the local Red Cross Branch. Their officials explained that, as they were a sister organisation to the St. John Ambulance Brigade, they must also refuse it. The money was then offered to the Oxford branch of the British Limbless ExService Men's Association who gratefully accepted it.

One effect of the local publicity was that I received letters from members of the public who wished to enquire about spiritual healing.

One lady wrote asking if she could receive healing although she was a Congregationalist. I visited her and found her living in very poor circumstances and suffering from nervous trouble. Her trouble appeared to be due to two main causes. Firstly, she was alone when one of her children was born and, secondly, one child, a boy, was a mongol who died in hospital during the war and she was concerned that he had not received the same care as normal children when he was in hospital.

I assured her that anyone could attend the weekly meetings for spiritual healing and that it was not important to what denomination they belonged. She attended and received benefit from the healing. At that time, a member of the church, who was developing mediumship, often used her psychic gifts at the healing meetings. Although she did not know the Congregationalist, she described a little boy whom she 'saw' clairvoyantly and the Congregationalist recognised her little mongol child from the description. She was amazed and uplifted by this event. The extraordinary sequel was that, after this particular meeting, I was walking home with both these ladies as our routes went in the same direction. During the conversation, the Congregationalist mentioned her fears about the treatment of her mongol child in hospital. Until then, the medium had not known the name of the Congregationalist. She had carried out nursing duties during the war and had actually nursed this little boy. She was able to assure the mother that her child had received the same loving care as normal children.

The fact of these two people meeting in a city as large as Oxford — the one able to supply the deep need of the other — seemed to me to be beyond the limits of coincidence and appeared to support the belief in guidance from the spirit world.

I saw no reason why people who had left the physical body

shouldn't be used for good works in the same way as those on earth.

In 1948, I had visited my mother in Shropshire and was returning to Oxford by train. When the train stopped at Birmingham, a young woman aged about 30 entered the compartment and sat in the corner seat opposite me. As the train went along I had a growing feeling that this young woman was in trouble and that I should help her. At first, I dismissed the idea but, later, in view of my belief in the possibility of guidance from the spirit world, I felt that I could not ignore it. By the time we reached Upper Heyford station the last of the other occupants of the compartment left the train. I then spoke to the young woman and told her about my impression. After a preliminary rebuff, she admitted that I was right and said that it was a case of divided loyalty. I felt that there was no need for details and I told her a few of the ideas I had learned about life. We soon reached Oxford and I told her that I was leaving the train and apologised for speaking to her on a personal matter. She gave me a beaming smile, thanked me, said that it had been most interesting and that she was sorry that I had to go.

I collected my bicycle from the station and, when riding from the station, found myself shaking my head and blowing through my mouth with a kind of shudder as though I was getting rid of something I had taken from her. Needless, to say, I was delighted that I had acted on the impression and that it had proved correct.

Whilst at Oxford, I contacted the secretary of the Oxford University Society for Psychical Research and he came and gave a talk on the work of the Society to our members.

Although I had been studying Spiritualism for some years, I had no means of judging my knowledge. I decided, therefore, to take a correspondence course known as the Speakers' Class B. Course. I found this very interesting and duly sat and passed the examination in due course.

The break-through of Spiritualism in America in 1848, its spread to Europe, its investigation by prominent men in science and religion during the nineteenth century was of great interest to me. It is not widely known that Sir William Crookes, a scientist with world-wide honours, was so convinced of the genuineness of psychic phenomena that he presented a paper on his investigations to the Royal Society in 1871. But his was a 'lone voice crying in the wilderness' and no serious notice was taken of it.

Several clergymen investigated psychic phenomena and wrote books on their experiences. Among these were the Rev. Charles Tweedale, the Rev. C. Drayton Thomas, the Rev. G. Vale Owen and the Rev. W. Stainton Moses who became the first President of the London Spiritualist Alliance (now the College of Psychic Studies) in 1884. Stainton Moses' most famous book was *Spirit Teachings* which is a record of spirit communications received in answer to his questions. The following extract appears in a communication concerning religion:

> The religion which we teach is one of acts and habits, not of words and fitful faith. We teach religion of body and religion of soul; a religion pure, progressive and true; one that aims at no finality, but leads its votary higher and higher through the ages, until the dross of earth is purged away, the spiritual nature is refined and sublimated, and the perfected spirit—perfected through suffering and toil and experience—is presented in glorified purity before the very footstool of its God. In this religion you will find no place for sloth or carelessness. The note of spirit-teaching is earnestness and zeal. In it you will find no shirking of the consequences of acts. Such shirking is impossible. Sin carries with it its own punishment. Nor will you find a convenient substitute on whose shoulders you may bind the burdens which you have prepared. Your own back must bear them, and your own spirit groan under their weight. Neither will you find encouragement to live a life of animal sensuality and brutish selfishness, in the hope that an orthodox belief will hide your debased life and that faith will throw a veil over impurity. You will find the creed taught by us is that acts and habits are of more moment than creeds and faith; and you will discover that that flimsy veil is rent aside with a stern hand, leaving the foul life laid bare, and the poor spirit naked and open to the eye of all who gaze upon it. Nor will you find any hope that after all you may get a cheap reprieve — that God is merciful, and will not be severe to mark your sins. Those human imaginings pale in the light of truth. You will gain

mercy when you have deserved it; or, rather, repentance and amendment, purity and sincerity, truth and progress will bring their own reward. You will not then require either mercy or pity.

It is not generally known that most Spiritualists subscribe to seven principles. These are:

1. The Fatherhood of God.
2. The Brotherhood of Man.
3. The Communion of Spirit and the Ministry of Angels.
4. The continuous existence of the human soul.
5. Personal responsibility.
6. Compensation and retribution hereafter for all the good and evil deeds done on earth.
7. Eternal progress open to every soul.

The similarity between the first and second principles and the following verses from St. Matthew 22 is very clear:

35. Then one of them, which was a lawyer, asked Him a question, tempting Him, saying,
36. "Master, which is the great commandment in the law?"
37. Jesus said unto him, "Thou shalt love the Lord thy God with all thy heart, and with all thy soul and with all thy mind.
38. This is the first and the great commandment.
39. And the second is like unto it. Thou shalt love thy neighbour as thyself.
40. On these two commandments hang all the law and the prophets."

Anyone reading these principles for the first time may well wonder what further link, if any, there is between Spiritualism and Christianity. One organisation, The Greater World Christian Spiritualist League, acknowledges the leadership of Jesus Christ.

The following further extract from spirit communications recorded by the Rev. W. Stainton Moses gives more information on this point:

It is our task to do for Christianity what Jesus did for Judaism. We would take the old forms and spiritualise their meaning, and infuse into them new life. Resurrection rather than abolition is what we desire. We say again that we do not abolish one jot or one tittle of the teaching which Christ gave to the world. We do but wipe away man's material glosses, and show you the hidden spiritual meaning which he has missed. We strive to raise you in your daily life more and more from the dominion of the body, and to show you more and more the mystic symbolism with which spirit life is permeated . . . The time will come when you will be able to see, as we cannot explain to you in your present state, the true dignity of man's higher life even on the earth sphere and the hidden mysteries with which that life is teeming.

Before you can reach so far you must be content to learn that there is a spiritual meaning underlying everything; that your Bible is full of it; man's interpretation and definitions and glosses being but the material husk which enshrines the kernel of divine truth . . . This was the mission of Christ, He claimed for Himself that fulfilment of the law, not its abolition or abrogation, was His intent. He pointed out the truth which was at the root of the Mosaic commandment. He stripped off the rays of Pharisaical ritual, the glosses of Rabbinical speculation, and laid bare the divine truth that was beneath all the grand principles divinely inspired which man had well-nigh buried. He was not only a religious but a social reformer; and the grand business of His life was to elevate people, spirit and body, to expose pretenders, and to strip off the mask of hypocrisy; to take the foot of the despot from the neck of the struggling slave and to make man free by virtue of that truth which He came from God to declare. "Ye shall know the truth", He told His followers, "And the truth shall make you free; and ye shall be free indeed".

He reasoned of life and death and eternity; of the true nobility and dignity of man's nature; of the way to progressive knowledge of God. He came as the Great Fulfiller of the law, the man who showed, as never man showed before, the end for which the law was given — the amelioration of humanity. He taught men to look into the depths of their hearts, to test their lives, to try their motives and to weigh all they did by the one ascertained balance — the fruits of life as a test of religion. He told men to be humble, merciful, truthful, pure, self-denying, honest in heart and intent; and He set before them a living example of the life which He preached.

The teaching of service to others is constantly received in spirit communications. The teachings received from Silver Birch, the spirit guide of the Home Circle of a well-known London journalist, Hannen Swaffer, have been published in several books. The following extract is typical of his philosophy:

> I am only concerned in the truth. The truth is all important. I am concerned only with service and helping your world to understand those spiritual, eternal principles on which a new world is being built. All those who deviate from that great task are frittering away energies which should be devoted to the service of their fellow-men and their fellow-women. The whole purpose of our return is to act as an incentive to all who will listen so that they can play their part in the regeneration of your world.
>
> Too much blind obedience is given to formulas. Too much attention is given to conventions. I am not concerned with anything but the spread of knowledge and the use of knowledge for the enlightenment of those who are still in darkness. I know only of one religion. It is service. Churches, buildings, creeds, doctrines, these do not interest me. We judge by action, by life, by motive. If those who have this knowledge are to succeed in the task, which is part of the plan, then they must be aware of imposing their own boundaries and attempting to restrict the flow of the power of the spirit into channels into which they think it should flow. The power of the spirit cannot be restricted or commanded. It flows wherever there are instruments through whom it can be expressed. We want instruments, mediums, men and women who will allow that power to touch them, who are so constituted that the voice of the spirit can be heard through them, and knowledge that is waiting to be transmitted can be poured through them. These are the urgent tasks.

This emphasis on service to others appears to me to link with the injunction by Jesus which is recorded in St. John 15:12, "This is my commandment, that ye love one another as I have loved you."

The fact of spirit communication helps one to draw a distinction between the mind and the brain. The mind functions through the brain. In some forms of brain damage which affect control of parts of the body, the mind is unable to function properly. This lack of function can be compared to an efficient typist who cannot be expected to produce first-class results if her typewriter has broken parts.

Most people who investigate Spiritualism claim that it gives them a deeper understanding of the psychic events recorded in the Bible and many feel that they have been misled by the church on psychic matters.

The Principle of Personal Responsibility usually gives people serious 'food for thought.' It emphasises the need for recognising that every thought, word and deed is creative and that its quality decides our spiritual progress. This calls for some personal soul-searching and, in many cases, some revision of daily habits. This Principle also agrees, of course, with the teaching in Galatians 6: 7, "Be not deceived; God is not mocked; for whatsoever a man soweth, that shall he also reap."

The following teaching by St. Paul in I Corinthians 12 is interpreted by Spiritualists as referring to various types of mediumship:

1. Now concerning spiritual gifts, brethren, I would not have you ignorant.
4. Now there are diversities of gifts but the same Spirit.
8. For to one is given by the Spirit the word of Wisdom; to another the word of knowledge by the same Spirit.
9. To another faith by the same Spirit; to another the gifts of healing by the same Spirit.
10. To another the working of miracles; to another prophecy; to another discerning of spirits, to another divers kinds of tongues; to another the interpretation of tongues.

At the same time, it is clear that the possession of psychic gifts does not necessarily make a person spiritual. Like everything else in life, it depends how such gifts are used. As a result of my experiences, I am convinced that a good living person can do more good with the help of psychic gifts.

The qualities required for mediumship vary as shown in the

following extracts from *Spirit Teachings* by Stainton Moses:

> Some are selected for the mere physical peculiarities which make them the ready vehicles of spirit power. Their bodily organisation is adapted for the purpose of manifesting eternal spiritual influence in its simplest form . . .
>
> Some are chosen because of their loving, gentle natures. In many cases they are not even conscious of communication with the spirit world, but they are the recipients of spirit guidance and their pure and gentle souls are cultivated and improved by angel superintendence . . .
>
> Others, again, are intellectually trained and prepared to give to man extended knowledge and wider views of truth. Advanced spirits influence the thoughts, suggest ideas, furnish means of acquiring knowledge and of communicating it to mankind . . .
>
> The most difficult task we have is to select a medium through whom the messages of the higher and more advanced spirits can be made known. It is necessary that the mind chosen should be of a receptive character. Moreover, it must be free from foolish, worldly prejudices. It must be a mind that has unlearned its youthful errors and has proved itself receptive to truth, even though the truths be unpopular. More still, it must be free from dogmatism. It must be free from the dogmatism of theologies and sectarianism and rigid creed. It must be a free and enquiring soul. It must be a soul that loves progressive knowledge and that has the perception of truth afar off. One that yearns for fuller light, for richer knowledge than it has yet received; one that knows no hope of cessation in drinking in the truth . . .
>
> We desire a capable, earnest, truth-seeking, unselfish, loving spirit for our work.

In view of the qualities required for mediumship, it seems extraordinary that, when discussing the work of the Churches' Fellowship for Psychical and Spiritual Studies with a local clergyman, he said, "Spiritualism is a pernicious thing!" The word "pernicious" is defined in the dictionary as destructive, hurtful, tending to injure or destroy. This is exactly the opposite of my personal experience.

I believe that my personal investigation into Spiritualism

strengthened my faith in God in a way in which the Church failed to do, despite my early upbringing.

The pioneer Spiritualists had almost as much opposition as the Tolpuddle Martyrs and many years were to pass before Spiritualism was accepted as a religion. This was mainly due to the efforts of Air Marshal Lord Dowding in the House of Lords.

The organised Spiritualist Movement has not progressed as much as one would expect but the steady growth of the National Federation of Spiritual Healers is significant. This body is composed mainly of Spiritualists and its members are now allowed to visit patients and give healing in many hospitals. Spiritual Healers believe that they are used as channels for the same divine healing power which operated through the disciples when, 2000 years ago, they were instructed to "Preach the Gospel and heal the sick".

It is common for reports in newspapers and magazines to refer to spiritual healers as faith healers. This seems to me to be a misnomer as successful results are obtained with animals, birds, babies and third parties for whom intercession has been requested without the patient being aware of this action.

Once the teachings of Spiritualism are accepted, there are many anomalies in daily life which confront one from time to time. The perpetuation of out-of-date phrases in the 'In Memoriam' notes are an example of this. The obscure references to 'Asleep in the Arms of the Lord,' and 'Called to Rest' are quite out of context with reality and an active new life in the spirit world. How sad it is to read verses like:

I lost my life's companion,
A life linked with my own.
God knows how much I miss him,
As I journey on alone.
He was a person very rare,
He loved his home, was always there.
He won't come back, we know it's true
But one day, dear, I'll come to you.

Death does not sever the bond of love and the loved one does return and draw closer but, in many cases, the mental barriers formed by ignorance hold him away.

Another problem which arises is that of the prophets. There are many references in the Old and New Testaments to the prophets and it is generally accepted that they were men inspired by God to uplift the people. It is natural that any thinking person must ask himself what has happened to them and to wonder where they are today?

According to the record in St. Matthew 23:37, Jesus said, "O Jerusalem, Jerusalem, thou that killest the prophets and stonest them which are sent unto thee". It is generally accepted that there has always been an enmity between the priests and the prophets and this attitude of mind may explain the events in the Middle Ages when thousands of witches or so-called witches were burned at the stake throughout Europe.

Communications from the spirit world refer to various spheres to which spirits gravitate as they earn the right and Spiritualists believe that these were referred to by Jesus when He said, "In my Father's house are many mansions: if it were not so, I would have told you" recorded in St. John 14: 2.

Whilst holidaying at Bournemouth with my wife, son and daughter, we became friendly with a lady staying at the same guest house who also had a son and daughter of about the same ages as our children. Her husband had been unable to accompany them as he had been taken ill just before the holiday. He died a few months later and his widow had to seek employment to maintain the family. When writing to me about this experience, she wrote, "I had the chance of quite a few posts during the last couple of weeks and have been very conscious of my beloved David's presence on many occasions, particularly when attending interviews, etc. He seemed to give me such poise and confidence and I therefore feel that we have him with us still and that he has only gone on before us. I am so grateful for this wonderful comfort."

A short while ago, in 1964, I mentioned details of a spirit communication to a small group of people and one of them, a devout Christian, questioned the veracity of this report saying, "Surely he (the spirit) should be at the right-hand of God?" This typifies the vagueness of orthodox teachings and it was heartening to me when, in the same year, I heard an enlightened clergyman say, "The Christian Church has made no clear pronouncement of life after death".

Most people attending Spiritualist services or seances have spirit guides described to them by mediums and I was no exception. In December 1958, I was leaving a medium friend after a short visit when she described a spirit with me. She thought that he was connected with automatic writing and described him as wearing old-fashioned clothes — a long light blue coat, dark blue breeches and light stockings. He had dark eyebrows, a strong aquiline nose and was wearing a wig. Although, at one stage, I had attempted automatic writing, I had not achieved any success. It is interesting however, that I have written verses from time to time since this experience. They have often been written for individuals and special occasions and have generally been well received. I had no interest in poetry at school and I have been intrigued by the variations in the phonetic endings of couplets which apparently evolved without any conscious effort on my part.

It may be that I act like a short-wave radio receiver in picking up the thoughts transmitted by the gentleman in old-fashioned dress and committing them to paper.

In 1951, I left Oxford to work at the Atomic Weapons Research Establishment at Aldermaston in Berkshire. By that time, I believed that personal guidance from the spirit world was operating in my life. I could not see any spiritual purpose, however, in this change and I carried on with my interest and joined the Spiritualist Church at Newbury in Berkshire, becoming an official for several years.

I met a young scientist once or twice who had a slight interest in psychic matters and I also met his wife. In December 1957, this young man was seriously injured as a result of an explosion in a laboratory and died four days later. This was indeed a real human tragedy! He had been happily married and, suddenly, his young wife was widowed and left with three children aged eight, five and one.

I visited the young widow from time to time and tried to help her by lending her books and telling her some of the philosophy which I had absorbed during my enquiries.

Although she left Newbury, I continued to keep in touch with her and the following extract from one of her letters indicates the degree to which she had responded to the deeper philosophy:

I have always had great difficulty in explaining what I feel but I am trying to thank you for what you have done for me. You have opened the doors and for that I am grateful. You told me that one's reactions to life's trials vary from people to people and, though I felt I had gained inner tranquility, others may emerge bitter and resentful of the way in which life had treated them.

It was with your help and patience that I learned to look beyond the narrow little world which I had built for myself. You guided me along the right path and so started the process which has led to the present state of mind.

I read a little of *In Tune with the Infinite* every evening. To know that we have the power within us to open or to close ourselves to the divine inflow exactly as we choose through the power of the mind and the operation of thought, and that in so doing we come into harmony with the highest, the most wonderful and the most beautiful and in the degree that we do this do we overflow so that all who come into contact with us receive the effects of this realisation on our part is truly amazing. I shall probably read this book twice — there is so much to absorb.

Already I can see the effects that the knowledge I have gained is having upon me.

I have never been a fearful person but I did fear death — not now, of course. Nor do I worry so much. I have always liked people — now I am learning to love them, to be more generous and not to be so critical.

The book *In Tune with the Infinite* was written by Ralph Waldo Trine and published in 1905. The frontispiece contains the following words: "Within yourself lies the cause of whatever enters into your life. To come into the full realisation of your awakened interior powers, is to be able to condition your life in exact accord with what you would have it."

In his book, *The Arcana of Spiritualism,* Hudson Tuttle wrote:

Nothing cannot originate something! If spirit has identity after death, then it must have a home, it must be organised.

The universe is undergoing a refining process. The spirit world is formed from the ascending sublimated atoms. To the perception of the clairvoyant, these ascending atoms are as plainly perceptible as is the ascent of vapour from water. They exhale from all substances.

The mineral mass, by the processes at work among its atoms, and the disintegrating chemical action of electricity and magnetism throws out ethereal particles into the great ocean of unindividualised spirit.

The plant, taking up crude mineral atoms, subjects them to a refining process in its interior cells and eliminates the finer particles.

The animal feeds on the vegetable and subjects it to a refining process ultimating a proportion of its atoms and exhaling them into the atmosphere. When the animal dies, the spiritual element of the wild animals escapes, as a drop of water evaporates, and mingles with the great ethereal ocean.

The spirit world is derived from these atoms. The spirit spheres surround the earth rather like the rings of the planet Saturn.

We are told that matter, when it first forms in the spirit world, is prone to assume the form in which it existed on earth. Hence, there are all the forms of life there as on earth, except those, such as the lowest plants and animals which cannot exist surrounded by such superior conditions. The scenery of mountain and plain, river, lake and ocean, of forest and prairie, are daguerreotypes of the same on earth. It is like earth with all its imperfections perfected, and its beauties multiplied a thousand-fold. It is a reflection of the earth and holds a close correspondence to it, but it can no more be compared with it in beauty than the finest miniature with the coarsest charcoal sketch.

The spirit holds the same relation to this spiritual universe that man holds to physical nature.

By an effort of will the spirit becomes positive to the place where it desires to go. Then there arises an immediate attraction to that place and it flies through the thin ether.

The sensualist, the depraved, in many instances, are so gross that gravity chains them to the earth's surface as it does man. They are denser than the spirit ether and hence have weight and cannot rise from earth. Others, who are more spiritual, can only rise to the first sphere; while others, still more refined, pass at will through the universal ocean of ether, visiting other globes and other solar systems . . . The degree of purity or spirituality determines whether or not the spirit shall be chained to earth or allowed freedom to travel the ocean of space.

The reason why we do not see spirits with normal vision can be compared with looking through a clear plate of glass or clear water. Although we do not see the glass or water because of the manner in which they transmit light rays, we do not disbelieve their existence . . .

The ideal of creative energy through all the vicissitudes of the past from the chaos of the beginning has been the evolution of a perfect man, that through him in a direct line might be evolved an immortal spirit.

Evolved from and by the forces of nature, being their concentration, or rather centrestantiation, man is an integral part of the universe. In him the history of the past is written. He is capable of comprehending all, because he is a part of all. In his mind are laid the orbits of solar systems and galvanic universes.

He makes grooves in which he compels the elements to run, by embodying his ideas in matter. All he does is the concretion of pre-existing thought. The engine — beautiful, perfect, a miracle of workmanship — the telegraph and the steamship, are ideas clothed with matter; embodied thoughts.

For a moment, lay aside all prejudices; let your religious education be as though it had never been; and calmly contemplate this being, with such antecedents, such universal relations, such boundless capacity and such destiny. Will you not scorn any system that offers violence and insult to the integrity of his character? Aye, trample underfoot the supposition that he is destined for anything but the unlimited progress of angel-life?

Such are the broad deductions of Spiritualism.

Man is not to be miserable on earth to enjoy heaven in the hereafter. We stand in the courts of heaven as much this hour, we see clearly the presence of God now, as we shall a thousand years hence. We are our own saviours. This is the religion of the future . . .

Spiritualism is the antagonist of Materialism. It stands for the science of life, here and hereafter; for the expression of the highest morality and the purest religion. The base of all religions is Spiritualism, our hope and evidence of immortal life rests on it.

If we believe there is a life after the death of the physical body; that such life is an infinite prolongation and evolution of this, that the spirit remains unchanged in being, that it may hold intercourse with those in this life, we are Spiritualists.

If we believe that this view of nature carries with it the highest, purest and most practical system of morals; that it is the basis of true religion, expressed in the loftiest phrases of self-forgetfulness in helping others, in noble living from the cradle to the grave, we are Spiritualists. If we refer to the fleeting changes called creation, from the expanding bud to the revolving sun, to force which thus being made cognizant in matter carries with it as a corollary that it is intelligent, loving and wise, planning for a purpose and pursuing a well-defined course to an end pre-determined, so pre-determined that even man with his finite mind often can calculate what it must be; if we place this power which is spirit in its infinite expression, then we are Spiritualists.

We must either be Spiritualists or Materialists. I prefer the former name. I not only prefer, but I am forced to accept it as the title of that system of philosophy by the cogency of facts which I cannot ignore.

It is not generally known that there is a small town named Palmelo in Brazil where all the inhabitants are Spiritualists. It has no police nor prison. It has schools, hostels, dispensaries and a hospital which was opened in 1953. It has one large temple but no churches of different religious denominations. It has become famous as a centre for spiritual healing and attracts annually hundreds of visitors suffering from incurable complaints. It is claimed to have records of outstanding successes with these patients. Each receives free treatment. One commentator describes Palmelo as a town with an atmosphere of great peace. Everyone is orderly, brotherly and charitable. There are no thieves or other kinds of criminals. It was founded by a farmer, Josino Branquinho, who settled there when it was a hamlet in 1929 and formed a small Spiritualist centre. A few years later, a well-known Brazilian Spiritualist also moved there.

An International Spiritualist Federation was formed in 1923 and holds a Congress every three years. Such Congresses have met at Liege, Paris, London, The Hague, Barcelona, Glasgow, Stockholm and Amsterdam. The first object of the Federation is "To strengthen Spiritualism as a world movement for the realisation of the spiritual nature of mankind."

V

ALDERMASTON

In November 1958, together with a few other members of the staff at the Atomic Weapons Research Establishment at Aldermaston, Berkshire, I helped to form the Aldermaston Society for Psychical Research. I was elected honorary secretary and, once again, an interesting pattern of events commenced which enlarged my mental horizons.

Looking back over the years, this event probably had greater significance than we realized at the time. As the fears of the terrible effects of atomic warfare grew in people's minds, these fears tended to be focussed on Aldermaston as the establishment was known to be concerned with the manufacture of atomic bombs. At certain national holidays, the people who took part in protest marches from Aldermaston to London drew attention to this. For several years, the numbers taking part in these marches increased to several thousands and, as details were naturally published in the national press and over radio and television, the publicity must have increased the link of fear in people's minds with Aldermaston.

Thoughts are things and, in psychic and spiritual terms, like attracts like. One can easily visualise, therefore, the large, dark "clouds" composed of negative thoughts of fear building up around Aldermaston.

It would be natural to assume that those in the spirit world who were working for the good of mankind would be well aware of this and that they would take counter-action so far as they were able to influence men and women who were suitable for the task. I have already referred to my belief in personal guidance from the spirit world and it is possible that I was telepathically impressed to choose to move to Aldermaston when I had the opportunity of either transferring to the Ministry of Supply or remaining in the Post Office. Whatever the cause, I feel sure that the existence of a Society for Psychical Research in an Atomic Weapons Research Establishment, which created the opportunity for reports of research into spiritual realms to reach, not only scientists and technicians, but also hundreds of thousands of local residents, must have had important repercussions. It may have been unique in the world. Every cause is followed by an effect and it is impossible to assess the full effects in the minds of those who attended our meetings or read of our activities.

It is a fact that I wrote over 40,000 words in reports on psychic matters which were published in the Establishment's monthly magazine, *A. W. R. E. News,* and that reports of semi-public meetings held in Reading were often published in five local newspapers with an estimated circulation of 150,000.

I had been aware for some years of the importance of the written word and believed that the mind faithfully records everything that is read, whether the full truth is absorbed at the time of reading or not. Believing also that there was a great need for spiritual enlightenment, it was easy for me to write the reports with almost monotonous regularity. It is obvious, of course, that there must have been a sequence of events which were interesting and worthy of report.

Members decided that the Objects of the Society would be, "The Study and Investigation of Psychic Phenomena and consideration of their Scientific and Philosophic Implications". The reference to the study of the philosophical implications was most important, in my opinion, as most people who carry out serious investigations into psychic phenomena find that the phenomena do occur and that the implications affect themselves and their attitude to life and other people.

We were fortunate in having the Establishment Technical Training Officer as our Chairman and our Scientific Adviser was a senior scientist who left Aldermaston later on to take a high government scientific post.

The Society developed naturally with arrangements being made for practical experiments, meetings with qualified speakers on a wide range of subjects and visits to seances, other groups, etc. In addition, a library was gradually formed and magazines were received regularly and circulated to members.

As secretary, I was in the happy position of corresponding with psychic researchers and also of observing the effect of the knowledge and experience on our members.

I was fortunate in receiving encouragement from well-known people. Dr. Raynor C. Johnson, Master of Queen's College, Melbourne University and author of contemporary books on psychical research wrote, "I am most interested to hear of the work your society is doing and send you my best wishes. I think it is very important that scientists, who are so impressively listened to today, and who are trained in scientific method, should investigate these things. The old materialism is slowly dying, I think, but its demise would be greatly hastened if sufficient scientists came out boldly with the facts they have observed and investigated and the conclusions they have been obliged to draw from them . . . You are certainly to be congratulated on the progress of the Society at Aldermaston and the research programme you have outlined".

Some sound advice and an offer of assistance was received from the well-known researcher, Dr. J. B. Rhine of Duke University,North Carolina, U.S.A.

Good wishes and advice also came from Professor C. D. Broad of Trinity College, Cambridge and also Professor C. W. K. Mundle of the Department of Philosophy, University College of North Wales, Bangor.

I was able to visit Professor H. H. Price, late President of the Society for Psychical Research and Professor Emeritus of the University of Oxford. He, too, was interested in the existence of our Society and offered his advice.

A direct link was also made with Professor Donald H. Andrews, Department of Chemistry, The John Hopkins University, Baltimore, U.S.A. In an article reporting his lecture given at the Rotary's Convention in Dallas, Texas in 1958, he is recorded as saying:

> The dominant power of the universe is not the shattering physical power of the atom. It is the power which lies beyond the material power of the atom in the unseen world of the music of the spirit — the power of love. It is this power, and this alone, which can guard us and guide us as we move forward into the awesome new world of atomics and automation, rockets and space.

The physical power of the atom is released by chain reaction. One atom explodes two, two explode four, four explode eight, until finally, the wave of explosion has released the total shattering power. Today, we need a chain reaction of the spirit to release in the world a new power of love. If only a few of us can have this vision and faith and have it intensely, we can be a torch which will start the chain reaction to ignite men's hearts throughout the world. We can open the doors to a golden future and, as the dawn of that new day brightens, we shall understand at last the meaning of the words, "The Truth shall make you free".

Mrs. Eileen J. Garrett, President of the Parapsychological Foundation, Inc., New York, when sending her good wishes and advice wrote, "The idea of promoting another Society in this day and age when everybody has so little time and not much money, demands a special kind of spiritual strength and purpose . . . May I wish you great success in the furtherance and advancement of your Research Society in this most needed and interesting subject".

The Parapsychological Foundation's brochure states that Parapsychology may be considered as the scientific inquiry into an area representing the common frontiers of philosophy, religion and science. The Foundation has encouraged parapsychological research in universities and by individual scientists in America and Europe and has also sponsored international conferences on the subject.

Some useful suggestions were received from Aldous Huxley from Los Angeles and also from Air Marshal Sir Victor Goddard who very kindly sent me a list of people whom he called "Metaphysical Scientists". In a later letter, he wrote, "Many congratulations on the progress of your Society. The first Society (other than a private group) which has approached the subject, so far as I know, with a positive scientific outlook rather than a mainly negative one".

I have always been disappointed that the Society for Psychical Research which has been in existence since 1882 and which has some excellent records on psychic matters, appears to hold no corporate views. A good example from the records of the Society is the case known as the "Palm Sunday Case". The case is so named because it refers to a young lady named Mary Catherine Lyttelton, who died on Palm Sunday in 1875, and her love story with Arthur, first Earl of Balfour, Prime Minister from 1902 to 1906. For thirty years after Mary Lyttelton's death about 3,000 scripts were written by about 12 scattered automatists of the highest integrity. These included Dame Edith Lyttelton; Mrs. Verrall, lecturer in classics at Newnham College, Cambridge; her daughter, Helen, later Mrs. W. H. Salter; Mrs. Fleming, a sister of Rudyard Kipling and Mrs. Winifred Coombe-Tennant, a well-known public figure. The scripts themselves claimed that three distinguished Cambridge Scholars, Professor Henry Sidgwick, Frederick Myers and Edmund Gurney who, in life, had been interested in the problem of survival and had recently died, had devised this method of demonstrating their continued existence and power to plan.

The chief investigators and interpreters of the scripts were Arthur Balfour's brother, Gerald (the second Lord Balfour), their sister, Mrs. Henry Sidgwick and a particular friend, Mr. G. J. Piddington. The early scripts, from 1901 to 1912, consist of cryptic allusive fragments written by Mrs. and Miss Verrall independently and by Mrs. Holland who lived in India. None of them appeared to know anything of the romance. Mrs. Holland came into the group because one of her scripts itself told her to send it to Mrs. Verrall's address in Cambridge. She did not know Mrs. Verrall or Cambridge and had never consciously heard of the address.

The Palm Sunday fragments, which were interspersed with many others, were meaningless taken alone but were ultimately considered by the investigators to make sense when pieced together after clues had been given. The first clues were disclosed in 1912.

In her review of the "Palm Sunday Case", Mrs. Rosalind Heywood, author of *The Sixth Sense,* wrote, "In the Palm Sunday scripts there is a mass of material which appears to hang together and which also convinced a group of highly intelligent investigators who gave many years to its study, that it referred to persons and events unknown to the scattered automatists who produced it. Given the characters of the persons concerned, conscious fraudulent collusion seems out of the question. Then can chance coincidence be stretched to cover it? If not, must we postulate extended extra-sensory collaboration between the subliminal minds of upright persons, to deceive the conscious minds of themselves and their friends? Or did it originate, as it claimed, with discarnate intelligence?"

It seems natural to me to expect a specialist society to give the general public information on the results of its investigations as the considered opinions of experts. In view of the importance of this subject and the general lack of knowledge of the 'man in the street' it would almost appear to be its duty.

The College of Psychic Studies, which was founded in 1884, performs an excellent function in maintaining a high standard in its lectures, etc., and it has a library of some 11,000 books. It has a Research Council and, in view of this, I felt that it was in an excellent position to give a lead to small groups of psychical researchers throughout the country. As the College has a number of mediums who are always available for private readings, etc., and most of its officers appreciate the need for providing the right psychological conditions to obtain good results from mediums, I thought that there were possibilities of forming good links with mediums and small amateur groups. The results could then be collated at the College and psychical research in Great Britain would be given a forward lift.

Although my motion at a general meeting of members at the College of Psychic Science was supported and carried, no effective action was taken by the Research Committee and I felt that it was this kind of negative attitude of mind to which Air Marshal Sir Victor Goddard referred in his letter.

An interesting comment on psychical researchers is contained in the following extract from *The Challenge of the Unknown* by Louis K. Anspacker:

> Let us consider the biological phenomenon called "histolysis" which we can observe in the spring in any garden. A caterpillar winds itself in its cocoon, its chrysalis. Then inside the cocoon occurs the amazing, stupefying process called histolysis. All the larval organs disappear! All the organs of the caterpillar are reduced to an amorphous, formless jelly, a sort of viscous emulsion, having no discernible structure. Then, by some miracle of reorganisation, directed by some mysterious dynamism, energised by some

obscure force, this formless and apparently dead emulsion transforms itself into the completed insect, a butterfly. It is now a thing with wings, adapted to an absolutely different environment, the air, and fitted for a totally different mode of life, as alien and remote from the crawling, factual, earth-bound life of the grub or caterpillar as are discarnate spirits, if there be any, to us in this life.

The old Greek word for butterfly is Psyche and the butterfly was, to the Greeks, the symbol of the soul.

Now, let us imagine a supernormal caterpillar, gifted with psychic powers, meeting an ordinary caterpillar and trying to explain histolysis or attempting to describe the unfettered, glittering and liberated life of the winged butterfly to the sceptical, commonsense, clubman caterpillar crawling contentedly on his undulating stomach and enjoying the cabbages of this world's garden. He'd say, "Oh, yeah, sure. That's alright if you like to believe it but, as far as my observation goes, this jolly conscious life of mind ends with my coffin, the cocoon. I don't know anything about wings but, just tell me, why do they have to make 'em in the dark?"

The geographical situation of Aldermaston, being out in the country, meant that staff travelled to work from the surrounding towns and villages covering a large area. This made the arrangement of local meetings of our society difficult. Nevertheless, we carried out practical experiments in telepathy, psychometry, radiesthesia, radionics, and table-tilting. Some results were obtained in each of these subjects and, as they were generally unexpected by those taking part, they often provided thrills. It was not easy, however, to find members with the spare time and faith to carry out experiments for a sufficiently long period of time to establish conclusive results.

The results in psychometry were obtained by recording a member's impressions received when holding a personal object belonging to an unknown member of the staff. The items would then be checked and marked. Scores of 6 out of 6, $18\frac{1}{2}$ out of 21, $20\frac{1}{4}$ out of 25, $11\frac{1}{4}$ out of 13 and $8\frac{1}{2}$ out of 12 were achieved. Some members achieved results without any previous experience in psychometry. One member, who was most persistent in his attempts, obtained reasonable results consistently and usually surprised members of the staff who were strangers to him and who had had no experience of psychic matters. It is interesting, too, that this member began to develop clairvoyance in view of the Spiritualists' claim that the practice of psychometry can develop clairvoyance. By the time I left Aldermaston, about 60 objects had been used and the results recorded.

Experiments in radiesthesia often proved interesting and surprising. A simple pendulum was used to detect a small article in the same way that a water diviner uses a hazel twig to detect water. There is no doubt that many people can get results with a simple pendulum but, like other faculties, considerable time and practice is required to obtain reliable results. A certain freshness of mind was found helpful in our experiments whereas boredom caused by repetition tended to reduce the standard of the results.

Interest was aroused by one of our public meetings when a man, who had been a member of the British Society of Dowsers for 24 years, demonstrated the use of the pendulum. He had used the pendulum to detect the radiations from underground streams which, he claimed, caused ill-health when they ran under houses. He also demonstrated how the pendulum could be used to determine the right food to eat.

Further information on the use of the pendulum was obtained from Mr. T. C. Lethbridge, author of *Ghost and Divining Rod*. In the preface of his book, Mr. Lethbridge wrote:

> Although I have been able to divine water, and do other simple things of that kind for many years, it never occurred to me that, with a little practice, I should be able to go to a given piece of turf, see the composition of many of the objects which lay in the soil beneath it, then dig it up and show that they were all there. When you can repeat an experiment again and again, it becomes a scientific experiment. Dowsing ceases to be a joke subject, it joins the world of facts.

Mr. Lethbridge worked out a system of rates relating to the length of thread required for the pendulum to react to a substance; e.g. 7" sulphur; 10" graphite; 12" carbon; 13" slate; concrete; 20" animals, plants, wood, coal, paper, etc.; 22" silver, lead; 26.5" running water; 32" iron. He had also plotted biconic fields of force and claimed that, with these further tables, it was comparatively simple to know the depth of an object hidden in the ground. Our experiments tended to confirm the results obtained by Mr. Lethbridge.

The pendulum is used by some doctors to diagnose illness and to aid the choice of homeopathic remedies.

In 1959, our Chairman met an amateur medium with strong psychic powers which became apparent after successful spiritual healing prevented his having an internal operation. The medium was a quiet, sincere man who was much more interested in philosophy than psychic phenomena and who sought no publicity but was rather at pains to avoid it.

Our Chairman and his wife became regular members of the medium's Home Circle and obtained first-hand experience of trance and physical mediumship. Our Chairman was invited by the spirit guides to take a camera and a rope to the seances. The rope was used to ensure that the medium did not get out of his chair during the periods when photographs were being taken. Precise instructions were given concerning the photographs and it was interesting that the complete spirit of co-operation with which our Chairman entered into the experiences evoked equal co-operation from the spirit guides and obtained worthwhile results.

Our Chairman gave an account of his experiences to our members which was reported in the June 1960 issue of the *A.W.R.E. News*. The report read:

> He gave a short account of his recent experiences in a small home circle with an amateur trance and physical medium. One of the most interesting of the physical phenomena was ectoplasm which had been demonstrated on several occasions. Photographs of it in various forms were shown to the audience. Other phenomena such as the levitation of a chair were also mentioned.
>
> Even more interesting were the individuals, about sixteen altogether, who spoke through the medium with clearly recognisable and distinctive voices. The sitters now know them as well as, if not better, than some of their friends in the flesh. On several occasions they answered questions which the sitters had discussed themselves but had not voiced to

the medium or his wife. He had found out that the technique of psychical research was different in many ways from that appropriate in physical research. By reacting to, and co-operating with, etheric communicators in the same way as one does with one's friends and colleagues, far more evidence can be obtained than if one adopts the critical and meticulous methods necessary when dealing with physical problems.

Physical phenomena, remarkable as they are, are comparatively uninteresting once they have been seen a few times. Far more interesting is the philosophy of this life, and the next as expounded by the principal communicator.

This last paragraph is all the more remarkable when, according to reliable reports I received, the power of the physical phenomena steadily increased until some of the spirit communicators were able fully to materialise and be seen by those present as vital, living people.

Extracts from the instructions and philosophy recorded on tape at some of the seances are printed below:

16th October 1959.

In all this communication with the spirit world there is only one real motive, that motive is to convince you that the earthly life is merely a minute part of eternal life and that there are other spheres which you must enter. It is with that object in view that we beg of you to give up your time and communicate with us to help show that light and to convince those people who walk in darkness that they are indeed wasting their time foolishly.

12th February 1960.

Before next week we shall have to have a bit of wiring done and have that red light there upon this side of the beam so that the light is not shining back into your camera but on to the curtain. Then you can dispense with the oil lamp. I think with the red light there, in the centre, shielded by the beam and all the lights forward plus a certain amount of light which we naturally produce, you should have some pretty good results.

26th October 1959.

The power of thought will reach the spirit world easier

than you can force it upon those on earth. We are aware of your spiritual needs.

30th October 1959.

Thoughts are things and as you think so your emotions radiate from that thought. For the sake of simplicity put those emotions into just two groups, love and hate. As you allow your thought to control those two emotions so all those around you are conscious of that vibration which is radiating from you, be the result happiness, be it on the other hand sorrow, nevertheless is it a fact, those around you and especially those who are near and dear to you are affected by those emotions. So, therefore, is it essential that you try always within yourselves to make sure that the thoughts which are within you are the thoughts of love. As that love radiates from you, you will find the mind stronger and becoming the constant home of thoughts which are good, thoughts which are true, thoughts of which you will never have any regrets or in any way be ashamed. Unless we have faith we cannot live and it is only by this fight of right against wrong that you get the peace of mind which is your heritage.

5th February 1960.

You see it is written in the Book — The Book of Truth — that book so often misunderstood, that if you throw your bread upon the waters, after many days it will return to you tenfold, a hundredfold. Now, of course, that does not mean bread — that is merely symbolic. Now, if you give, you will receive and, according to the motive and the strength which you give so it is returned unto you a hundredfold, a thousandfold.

Sometimes you ask why it is just a few who have understanding offered to them, who have a light offered to them, who have a chance to understand the future? Well, again in the Book, you read of the wise virgins and the foolish virgins. Now there are many foolish ones, they are too selfish, they are too wrapped up in their worldly goods and worldly life to worry about preparing for the future. Now, preparing for the future does not mean that you neglect the living of your earthly life, but your spiritual life is wrapped up in your earthly life, and instead of being foolish it is much more easy to be wise and to prepare yourself for that which lies beyond — to understand it.

No-one who has sought has sought in vain yet. There will come a day when these people will need it and want it, then is the time for you to sow your seed, then is the time to throw out your bread; but you cannot make someone believe something which they are not ready to believe. But there does come a time in everyone's life when they are ready, there is a time in the seasons when the soil is ready and ripe for the seed, so it is with the lives of people.

The time when they ask is the time to concentrate. The greatest way to get them is by example. When they see that you have something which they lack, when they feel coming from you that life which they cannot understand, there is nothing like a mystery to make people curious, to draw them, and once they see and feel that coming from a person and then, when the time comes and they realise that they are in darkness, they are empty, that their lives are getting them nowhere, well, then is the time they seek. But, still, it is not of any avail if they seek from a selfish motive and are not prepared to seek for seeking's sake.

12th February 1960.

Always remember in your life, always, that there are two things — positive and negative. Now, if you are positive, you succeed. If you are negative, you fail. If, in between those two, you allow any doubt to come, well, things can be very painful because you must always remember that doubt is the canker, the cancer of the mind. If you are positive, there is no doubt. If you are positive you have faith. If you have faith, you live. If you live, you succeed.

26th February 1960.

Now, with all kinds of growth from the beginning to perfection, be it plant or animal, or anything. We start from, shall we say, the seed. Let's take the, oh, the oh so common oak tree. Now, you cannot get lovely carved furniture made of solid oak before the process from the acorn unto perfection has taken place, can you? Now this which you seek, we know all about it. It is something which you cannot adequately explain even to yourself. Let me tell you now that it would be impossible for you to know and understand that which you seek all in a flash. In the beginning you, say, get the feeling that you want to know something and then you get interested, and then you begin to understand a little, such a teeny, weeny little. Well, that teeny, weeny little cannot grow into the full understanding which you seek immediately. It would be altogether too much for you, but you will find that, as you progress along, unknown to you, you will not find the visible measurements of so many yards a day or so many pounds a day — you cannot measure it. But, gradually, and this is the only way, it is the perfect way and it is the correct way. The seed was sown in your mind and you were honest enough with yourself to seek. Having sought and been offered just a tiny, weeny spark of light, you begin to seek further and, as you progress, let me tell you for quite a while you will still have that feeling of wanting to understand more, but do believe me when I tell you that because you cannot understand all at once that you are lacking in any way because it must be like that. There must be all the stages of progress, all the different periods of time if knowledge must sink into you and the only true people, the only people who really enjoy life, who lead a full life, who really understand life, are those willing to let this knowledge grow its natural way. And, growing in a natural way it becomes a part of you. It is not something which you have to try and believe, to try and hold. You will find it will not be like that. It will be a part of you, it will be of you, it will be you. And it will be as natural for you to know these things and to understand them as it is for your feet to go to the ground and go one in front of the other when you want to walk, for you to listen when you want to hear, for you to speak when you want to voice. All the things which you do, the natural things, the things which have become a habit will be linked unto this knowledge which you seek, it will become a part of you, a natural part. You will not then wonder why. If you wonder why at all it will be only why didn't you understand before, but you need not worry about that because it is getting to know. One tree grows up in a few years, reaches completion and, its mission accomplished, it dies. Another one takes years and years and years. All of you are different and it is only the fact that you are different that you have to find out in different ways. If you get a different feeling about these things it is because it comes to you differently.

You will find that it will become part of you and that is the way, the only way, for you to be able to appreciate life, for you to build your soul into a character, a lasting character which will carry that life, that fire, that understanding from the earth state into the etheric. Do not worry because you cannot understand everything at once. Actually you do, within yourself, within your mind, understand already much more than your conscious self realises. But seek, yes, still seek. Ask and it will be given unto you. We know, we understand, but we cannot live your life for you, but we still have to leave you to come along alone. We can take your hand and help you over the rough spots but still it must be you, the real you, the only you, on your own efforts who will live the life which is yours, otherwise we would take away your free-will. That would not be right. The greatest crime that anyone can do is to take away the free-will of another. You may maim the body, you may destroy the body but to take away their free-will is a far greater crime.

The value of the report on this medium rests on the testimony of, and recordings made by, a man of undoubted integrity combined with scientific training.

One wonders how many other similar cases there are in the country of amateur mediums who prefer to remain anonymous rather than be bullied and badgered by all the sceptical "Doubting Thomas's" who, unfortunately, appear to form the majority of any community.

A lecture which aroused much interest among our members and friends was that on Acupuncture which was given by a doctor. Acupuncture is claimed to be one of the oldest forms of medical art and is said to have been in use in China 5,000 years ago. It was also used in Egypt and Mexico.

The treatment is based on the belief that the 12 basic organs of the body are connected with the thumbs, fingers, toes and head by meridians of energy. Practitioners, after extensive training, become so sensitive in the fingers that they can diagnose which of the 12 main organs are diseased by taking a pulse diagnosis. They then treat by sticking gold and silver needles 1/10" into the skin and leaving them in place for five or fifteen minutes.

Acupuncture is stated to exert its influence via the automatic nervous system. An impulse travels along some fibres of the nervous system to the brain and then to the organ concerned. The regulating effect of the nerve fibres in the organ cause the appropriate changes necessary to repair the diseased tissue, a dilation of the capillary blood vessels of the organ causing more blood, oxygen, hormones, etc., to be brought to it, thus effecting a cure.

The meridians of energy are said to follow the embryological twist. They cannot be traced anatomically but trained practitioners are said to be able to perceive the cosmic etheric force streaming into acupuncture points of the body. It is described as a finely streaked bluish-white light in the shape of a slight cone. Within about two inches of the skin this force suddenly becomes invisible. It is claimed that the force is transformed from a cosmic etheric to a terrestrial human etheric force. Some people claim that the acupuncture points have a reduced electrical resistance which can be detected by instruments.

The cycle of energy is said to start at 3 a.m., a time when many babies are born and a time following a period when many people die or have crises in illnesses.

An interesting claim, which is also made by Radionic practitioners, is that pre-clinical states of disease can be diagnosed.

A lecturer spoke of the Chinese monistic conception of life and the fact that their ancient literature did not distinguish between the material and the non-material. They linked psychological conditions with internal organs such as Depression — Liver, Fear — Kidneys, Anguish — Lungs, Obsession — Spleen and Joy — Heart. It is claimed that the treatment of the internal organ clears the relevant psychological condition.

Acupuncture is included in the Chinese medical curriculum and is practised by half a million modern Chinese doctors. There are several thousand doctors practising it in Europe and it is taught in four universities in Russia.

The romantic story of the Kahunas of Polynesia was the subject of another interesting lecture.

At one time, there were twelve tribes of the Kahunas living in the Atlas Mountains in North Africa. They moved to the valley of the Nile where they built the Pyramids and controlled Egypt.

Because of their ability to foretell the future, they were aware that there would be a time of great intellectual wilderness so they decided to emigrate. Eleven of the tribes set off to islands in the Pacific and one tribe returned to the Atlas Mountains. The lecturer stated that there are still eleven tribes of Polynesians with different dialects.

The Kahunas believed that man is, first of all, a triple unity in a physical body — the low self or subconscious, the seat of memory; the middle self or conscious which has no memory but full reasoning powers and the higher self or superconscious, the divine part of man. The low self is like the highest form of domestic animal. It is attached to the middle self like a brother and collects and stores vital energies for all the selves. The middle self has the task of educating the low self and helping it to evolve. The higher self is like an utterly trustworthy parental spirit. It is evolved beyond our comprehension, it can see into the future to a degree and can carry out instant healings. The recipients of such healing have to be completely free of any guilt complexes and fully imbued with faith. The philosophy of the Kahunas was not to hurt anyone but to help and love whenever possible.

The Kahunas could walk barefoot on lava only just solidified sufficiently to bear the weight of a man, they could foretell the future and sometimes change it, they could perform instant healing and control the winds, weather and man-eating sharks.

The lecturer considered that a study of the powers used by the Kahunas could perhaps explain extra-sensory perception and psychic phenomena.

Many members of the public may associate Yoga with a facility to stand on one's head for long periods. A lecture on Yoga extended our knowledge on this subject and proved so popular that it was repeated. The lectures included demonstrations of some of the postures which are used by the followers of Yoga.

The word "Yoga" is derived through the Sanscrit, from the

same Indo-European root as the English "to yoke". It can also be translated as "union" or "identification". This "union" is the merging of the individual soul with the universal soul.

Yoga developed among nomadic tribes who settled in India about 3,000 B.C. Some members could not accept the personification of God taught in the Hindu religion. They broke away and formed the first community of seekers (Yogis) in an endeavour to find their own Pathway of life. They practised Karma Yoga by performing some service to the community in the hope of being given meals. They tended not to kill their herds as they had a natural reverence for life and were vegetarians. They tried to keep themselves physically fit.

Rajah or Royal Yoga is concerned with control of the mind and the emotions, keeping on an even keel mentally, not allowing the dissipation of energy by odd and random thoughts.

Bhakti Yoga is the Yoga of spiritual meditation, spiritual steps to achieve fulfilment and enlightenment.

Mantra Yoga aids the concentration of the mind by sound vibrations, repeated chanting and the repeating of couplets and words having spiritual meaning.

Hatha Yoga teaches the mastery of the body by means of postures which tone up the nervous system and the internal organs by increasing the flow of venous blood so that it is replaced by fresh oxygenised blood.

It is not surprising that Hatha Yoga is becoming increasingly popular in the West. The system does not aim at developing just muscular strength or size but the health and efficiency of the internal organs. Also, it does not require any special apparatus and a quarter of an hour's daily practise can produce beneficial results.

The Plough posture is claimed to:

(1) Promote suppleness of the spine and help to maintain its natural curve.
(2) Tone up the nervous system.
(3) Stretch and make more supple almost all the body muscles.
(4) Exercise the abdomen and prevent disorders of the stomach.

(5) Improve the circulation and send a rich flow of blood to the spine.

(6) Be one of the best movements for normalising the obese figure and to rejuvenate the whole body.

Those who are interested in finding out more about the deeper spiritual teaching of Yoga may be inspired by the following extract from, *The Heart of the Eastern Mystical Teaching* by Hari Prasad Shastri. The book is said to present the life of practical Yoga as revealed and lived by the Saint Shri Dada of Aligarh:

> When a purified mind, divested of its load and selfishness, comes into contact with the Universal Mind by meditation, its thoughts will bear fruit at the right time, like seeds sown in carefully tilled soil.
>
> Happiness depends on two factors — forgetfulness of narrow egoity and illumination of the vacuity in the mind caused thereby.
>
> Live in such a way that men may honour the memory of your father in you.
>
> Make simple living your rule and do your duties selflessly.
>
> Educate your desires, cultivate your mind and know that God sees you throughout the twenty-four hours. Please Him with your love and loving service to His children.
>
> Love of abstract principles like truth, compassion, benevolence, philosophy, science and history is a higher kind of love. But you have to cultivate this love and foster it by keeping the company of similarly-minded people.
>
> Love of family is not an end in itself. Each member of a family, while loving other members, must love art, poetry and music and kindle the flame to the Lord in his heart.
>
> Selfish motives deprive any desire, however worthy, of spiritual value.
>
> Our senses read matter, mind reads the mind. Spirit is the heavenly force which measures the functions of the mind and gives a direction to them if the mind endeavours to still itself and approaches the spirit.
>
> Work to create harmony in society.
>
> Worship will give you equanimity and courage, which are your greatest friends in the world.

Your daily bread will be sweeter if you share it with your friends and with those less fortunate than you.

A lecture on Telepathy was given by Dr. S. G. Soal, a former Senior Lecturer in Pure Mathematics at London University, a former President of the Society for Psychical Research and author of *Modern Experiments in Telepathy* and *The Mind Readers*.

Dr. Soal outlined experiments carried out in Telepathy since the word was coined in 1882. He commenced tests in 1934 and tested 160 people over 5 years with 128,350 guesses. He found that the results were the equivalent of chance. However, another researcher named Whateley Carrington suggested that he should re-examine his results. He did so and found that two of his percipients had been making good scores, one on the following card and the other on the card immediately before and after the target card. Dr. Soal then carried out extensive tests with the two successful percipients — Mr. Shackleton and Mrs. Stewart. On one occasion the odds in 200 trials against Mr. Shackleton's correct hits occurring by chance were more than ten million to one. (When attending a meeting in London, I met Mrs. Stewart and found her a sincere, homely type of person).

Dr. Soal also described his tests with two Welsh boys from Capel Curig. They obtained results above those of chance and these became higher when monetary prizes were awarded for higher scores.

When Mrs. Muriel Hankey, Principal of the College of Psychic Science, Ltd., London visited our Society, she told us that the College received a large amount of correspondence from overseas. It also had visitors from America, Australia, New Zealand and all parts of Europe, especially Scandinavia. On one occasion, a visitor from Iceland received Icelandic names and expressions from a medium who had no knowledge of the language.

Mrs. Hankey described how, during a visit to Mexico, a London medium was taken to the area of the excavacated ancient temples of Mitla, Oaxaca. The medium was entranced and spoke in the dialect of the Zapotec Indians which was translated by the Indian guide.

Air Chief Marshal Lord Dowding, G.C.B., G.C.V.O., C.M.G.,

described many of his experiences in investigating psychic phenomena when he spoke to the Society.

He spent some time with a small group who specialised in helping R.A.F. men who, because of the circumstances of their sudden deaths, were not fully aware of their new surroundings. He related one incident when a bomber crew of seven entered their room and "wandered" around it without being aware of Lord Dowding and his friends. On being told by the medium that one of the crew had approached the piano, Lord Dowding went to it and opened the lid whereupon the lad said, "Gosh! This place must be haunted".

Lord Dowding also described seeing materialised spirit forms when a lady materialised, carried a small table with paper on it across the room to him and signed her name twice before dematerialising.

In October 1960, five members of the Society attended a seance at Newbury given by the well-known physical medium, William Olsen of Sheerness. The following extracts are taken from a report written by a technical member of the Society who attended the seance:

> Two volunteers searched Mr. Olsen while his jacket was being passed around for inspection. The medium, having put on the jacket, another volunteer sewed the jacket together. A colleague and I securely tied the medium by the arms and legs with cord to an armchair. We formed a circle and were "hand-cuffed" together with strong elastic bands and were requested to keep holding hands throughout the seance . . .
>
> Two megaphones floated into the air and commenced racing around the circle just missing our heads. Subsequently, I was informed that the table took the same path. I am thankful that I was unaware of this at the time! The megaphones then commenced to execute a variety of manoeuvres, just missing each other but sometimes touching the ceiling. Their movements could easily be followed as they had been painted with luminous paint . . .
>
> Several people, including one of our members, received messages and frequently one heard the voice of a young child speaking to a relative. A voice then mentioned that several

dogs were present. I immediately thought of my dog and promptly called his name. The megaphone, which was then on the opposite side of the circle, came across the floor like a rocket, with one bound, landed on my lap barking and pressing itself against my face as if to lick me. The total impression caused by the weight, the bark and the terrific excitement which was communicated to me made me feel certain that it was Pat. I also noticed that the barks of the other dogs claimed by their owners were different . . .

The next manifestation occurred when the red light grew brighter showing the medium seated in his chair with ectoplasm extending from his chin to his feet. It then stretched out rather like a tube onto the floor. At the same time, his jacket was seen to slip off onto the floor. The lamp extinguished and, shortly afterwards, there was a loud thud within the circle. This was followed by a manifested voice saying a prayer. The general lighting was then switched on and the medium was seen seated in the centre of the circle still tied to his chair. We immediately examined the cords and found the knots intact just as we had tied them! The jacket was inspected and the stitching found to be in place. We helped the medium to another room where he was provided with tea. He appeared to be still only semi-conscious.

I was not present on that occasion but I have attended similar seances given by Mr. Olsen on five or six occasions. I have seen ectoplasm, heard the voices and also the barks of a dog although there were no physical dogs in the room. Mr. Olsen has been visiting Spiritualist Churches throughout the country for many years and is regarded by church officials as a genuine physical medium.

In connection with physical phenomena, it is interesting to recall the Report on Spiritualism made by the London Dialectical Society which was published in 1871. Six sub-committees tendered reports, one of which held forty meetings of investigations over a period of a year. One experiment demands attention. Eleven members of the sub-committee, none being a professional, placed chairs around a heavy dining room table, backs of chairs towards the table and eighteen inches from it. In full gaslight the members then knelt on the chairs with faces towards the table and hands clasped behind their backs. Under these conditions the table moved thirteen times in various directions, sometimes according to the request of members.

The Committee's Report recorded:

> 1. Sounds of varied character apparently proceeding from furniture, floors and walls occur without being produced by muscular or mechanical contrivances.
> 2. Movements of heavy bodies take place without contact or connection with any person.
> 3. Sounds and movements occur at the times and in the manner asked for by persons present and by simple code answer questions and spell out coherent communications.
> 4. The presence of certain persons seems necessary to phenomena and of others adverse.

A link was established with Dr. C. C. L. Gregory, Editor of *Cosmos,* the magazine of the Institute for the Study of Mental Images. In the March, 1963 issue of *Cosmos,* when commenting on the book, *Experiments in Mental Suggestion* by L. L. Vasiliev and the Russian approach to this kind of research, Dr. Gregory wrote:

> Both in this country and in the U.S.A. a great deal of ingenuity has been expended on systematically ignoring or decrying, often on the flimsiest pretexts, all evidence, both past and present, for all paraphysical phenomena, even when vouched for by living members of the Committee of the Society for Psychical Research.
>
> Professor Vasiliev has described in great detail his work on some correlations between the behaviour of a few special subjects in special states or conditions and directed mental activities of distant persons up to a distance of 1700 kms. What he eventually succeeded in doing for the first time in 80 years of psychical research was to demonstrate telepathic phenomena with sufficient reliability and repeatability to make possible a further investigation.
>
> Naturally, non-Soviet scientists will be eager to know what (apart from Vasiliev's experimental genius and devotion) were the conditions that we have lacked, so that they were successful where we have failed.

It seems to us that the most important single factor was that the Soviet scientists were both continually subjected throughout the entire work to the most searching, well-informed and constructive criticism by critical scientific specialists in a number of relevant fields, while at the same time the investigators were protected (so far as one can tell) from the type of persecutions that makes any serious scientific investigations in the West into such matters practically impossible.

Vasiliev has evidently been working under what might be called conditions of monastic discipline in which his superiors and colleagues were able and willing to subject his work throughout to the severest criticism, and indeed eventually all this work was kept secret for a quarter of a century, presumably owing to the adverse effects of world warfulness on fundamental scientific investigations. In return for this quasi-monastic discipline he was protected from smears, threats and personal injury, so that when the ban was lifted he was still in a condition to complete the work and publish a first-class account of it. It is to be hoped that all Western scientists will take this to heart and compete with Soviet scientists who are now apparently interested in the question of the energetic nature of mental suggestion.

Psychical Research, as it has been known for the last near-century, has now collapsed in a welter of scandal, gossip, double-talk, inquisitorial chicanery, business racket, proselytising and nonsense generally — and not because the alleged phenomena do not happen. The principle reasons for its collapse are twofold: the attempt to provide evidence for supposed facts that are at variance with the whole structure of scientific convention and pre-supposition without altering these conventions was doomed at the outset. The other major reason is the involvement of the subject with religion and politics.

Having been in existence for over five years, it was inevitable that the Society at Aldermaston would attract some publicity. A feature about the Society was published in the national weekly magazine *Today*, dated 27th July 1963. As usual, this resulted in letters arriving from complete strangers. One letter came from a Mr. J. S. Blackhall, a retired electrical engineer living in Northern Ireland. He claimed to have been carrying out psychical research for forty years, that he had developed some equipment so that spirit communicators could cause an electric bell to ring when they wished to contact him and that he had developed the use of super high frequencies for healing purposes. He claimed that these frequencies ranged up to 3,000 million Mc/s whereas the highest frequencies known to man were 30,000 Mc/s.

Mr. Blackhall died in 1963 and 10 of his notebooks containing full details of his research were sent to me. The contents of the notebooks are now being investigated.

VI

GRACE ROSHER AND SIR WILLIAM CROOKES

One of the most interesting speakers at our meetings was Miss Grace Rosher of London. Miss Rosher had had no interest but rather a distaste of anything of a psychic nature and was a devout church member. In September, 1957, she was used for automatic writing which purported to be controlled by her fiancé, Gordon Burdick, who had "died" fifteen months previously. The writing developed and was examined by the Rev. G. Maurice Elliott, General Secretary of the Churches' Fellowship for Psychical and Spiritual Studies. He arranged for the writing to be compared with original letters from Gordon Burdick by a professional graphologist of sound repute. In his conclusions the expert wrote, "From a comprehensive assembly of twenty dominant, conscious and unconscious writing tendencies and movements in the original scripts, no less than sixteen of these tendencies appear in the reproduced writing . . ."

Miss Rosher's experiences and detailed reports of the communications received from Gordon Burdick were published in her book *Beyond the Horizon*. This book was sponsored by The Churches' Fellowship for Psychical and Spiritual Studies and, in his introduction to the book, Canon J. D. Pearce-Higgins wrote "Those who accept these communications as genuine information need not be unduly cast down by the communicator's lack of theological knowledge, for they will only see in this confirmation of what have always been tenets of the Christian faith, first that in the Father's house in the hereafter are many mansions — i.e. many degrees and planes of consciousness, and secondly that the ministry of God's angels or messengers is indeed a reality. It is indeed a comforting thought to believe that the Heavenly Civil Service, if I may call it so, is working overtime on our behalf, on behalf of all men of good will to still the madness of the nations and to avert the catastrophe which we all dread, and towards the prevention of which Gordon Burdick would appear so solemnly to call us to exert ourselves to the utmost."

At first the pen was held in a loose grasp, then it wrote just leaning against Miss Rosher's clenched fist. Later on, it wrote leaning against her forefinger and Gordon Burdick expressed the hope that, eventually, he would be able to use the pen without any support.

In one communication Gordon Burdick wrote:

> If people were taught that by the way they act and think and use their God-given abilities in their earthly life they were building up their future for good or ill in the "Hereafter", as we call it, they would pay less attention to the things of the material world. I do not think that the religions teach enough about this other world and so much that they do teach is so far from the truth as to be merely silly, so silly, that no thinking person bothers about it and dismisses the thought of what will happen to him after his period of life on earth is over from his mind altogether, or adopts a "wait and see" attitude, assuming that it doesn't really concern him very much. He has enough to do coping with this world to bother about the next. That is the attitude of a vast number of people especially business men. What is needed is to impress on people that life on earth is a preparation for life hereafter; we make our own heaven and hell which are not places exactly, but states of consciousness, by the way we use our gift of life on earth. It is such a pity that so few people seem to realise this. It is because I have had to deal with just this problem in my work over here, that I feel so deeply about it. It would save so much unhappiness and regret on this side if only people were more informed as to what awaits them in their future life.

I asked Miss Rosher if we could submit questions to Gordon Burdick and she agreed. When Gordon Burdick wrote that he would get a scientist to answer them, Miss Rosher was surprised that the scientist was said to be Sir William Crookes. She knew some members of the Lodge family and, therefore, assumed that the scientist would be Sir Oliver Lodge. I was not surprised because I had made particular reference to Sir Willam Crookes at the inaugural meeting of our society and we believed that he had spoken to a small group of officials of our society when we visited a well-known London medium, Leslie Flint, in January 1960.

In May 1960, Gordon Burdick wrote, "I have William Crookes here to answer those questions." The questions which we submitted and the answers given were:

Qn. At what frequency would it be possible for mortal man to communicate with the spirit world, assuming some normal form of radio transmitter were used? If possible, please express the frequency in megacycles or, if in wavelengths, in metres or centimetres.

Ans. It would not be possible to get in touch with the world we inhabit with any radio transmitter in present use in your world. It will require a transmitter of greater power which will no doubt in due course be invented because the wavelength is of such a high speed that it cannot be measured in either centimetres or millimetres — it will be in trillimetres.

Qn. Could you express the frequency in megacycles?

Ans. No. It would be a frequency much higher and faster than the megacycle units in the light waves in radiation from your sun. The cycles would be far greater in number to the second than anything at present known on your side.

(At this point Miss Rosher wrote, "I asked what a megacycle was as I had no idea what it could be. I looked for it in the dictionary but couldn't find it. I asked my brothers but they couldn't tell me off-hand. So I asked first G.B. and got the answer that it was a "million wave movements rotating at tremendous speed in a constant pattern." Not being satisfied with that information, I asked again when Crookes was supposed to be the communicator through G.B. The answer I got this time was, "A megacycle is a measurement of a frequency which has a million rotations to the second" and that it was, "related to the highest frequencies known to earth on the present scale of measurements." This, I decided, was sheer nonsense and did not proceed with the communications on that occasion because I thought I was just getting nonsense! Later on, asking Mr.

Livens of the M.S.A. (Marylebone Spiritualist Association) if he knew what a megacycle was, to my surprise, he gave the same answer!")

Qn. What frequency is used in telepathic communication between
(a) The spirit world and mortal man?
(b) Mortal man and mortal man?

Ans. The frequency used in telepathic communication between mind and mind either in the spirit world or on earth or between earth and the spirit world is of the same frequency and is a non-material wave but similar to light or radio in one sense but is of a higher frequency than any material wave, that is, a wave which it is possible for those on the physical plane to operate with.

Miss Rosher had thought that the answers were nonsense and she did not send them to me immediately. After receiving confirmation from Mr. Livens, however, she decided to repeat the questions and did so on the 1st July 1960 with the following results:

Qn. At what frequency would it be possible for mortal man to communicate with the spirit world assuming some form of radio were used? If possible, please express the frequency in megacycles or, if in wavelengths, in metres or centimetres.

Ans. It would not be possible to establish communications with the world we now inhabit through any radio transmitter in use in your world at present. No doubt, in due course, a more powerful instrument will be produced which will make contact possible. It would require a more powerful instrument because the wavelength would be much shorter than anything so far discovered by you and is beyond the ordinary scale of measurements. The frequency would not be counted in megacycles as it is of still greater speed and is approximately that of mental or thought communication which is of a higher frequency than any physical or so-called material wave — that is, of a wave measurable in physics.

Qn. Can you help the scientists anxious to make contact with your world in any way? If it is a psychic force at what speed does this radiation travel? If possible, give the answer in metres per second or miles per second.

Ans. In any of the forces called psychic it is not possible to give measurements in either time, speed or distance for time and space as understood on the physical plane no longer exist. Therefore, it will only be possible to contact this world through a non-physical wave similar to that which operates in thought force which governs all activity on this other plane of conscious life. This is a world controlled and governed by mind with a capital M and what is most likely to happen is that the connecting link will be stumbled upon on your side. We on this side are working to that end.

Qn. Any more?

Ans. Yes. It is only through mental or thought transference that we can guide those who are seeking to get into communication with this other state of consciousness. We are doing our utmost in this direction and we are even more anxious than you are to make the break-through. We can only do so through mental suggestion and hope that some mind which is sufficiently attuned will receive the information we are trying to give and be able to act on it.

18th August 1960.

Qn. What is a trillimetre?

Ans. A trillimetre is a measurement of a wavelength at present beyond the scope of instruments for measurement on earth. It is a wavelength whose velocity and frequency is nearer that of this next sphere which is only just within the possibility of measurement on the earth plane.

Qn. If it is not possible to give the answer in units employed on earth, is the frequency of telepathic communication greater than 3×10^{27} cycles per second?

Ans. Yes it is. The frequency, which is connected with all our mental activity on this other plane of activity on this other plane of experience, is higher even than that, in fact is beyond measurement as understood on earth. But in order for communication to be established with earth there will need to be a different standard of measurement employed.

These questions were asked by Miss Rosher.

Qn. What do you mean?

Ans. I mean that the scale of measurement at present known to earth is not ultimate.

Qn. Would it then, the frequency, be higher than that of cosmic radiation?

Ans. Yes.

Qn. Why?

Ans. Because we live in a sphere beyond the limits of cosmic radiation which is connected with the physical universe. It will be possible to make contact eventually but not with the instruments in present use.

Qn. Why?

Ans. Because you must realise that the energy expressed in units on earth is lower than the energy which is the source and governing factor of spiritual life. This term refers to the nature of life no longer governed by physical laws.

William Crookes.

On the 30th January 1961, Miss Rosher received the following communication in a copper-plate style of writing, very different to the rounded style of Gordon Burdick:

I would like to say that it is most important that those men of science who wish to link up with scientists on this side should make a study of the science of metaphysics which goes beyond mathematical measurements and is, from our point of view, true science. Science is the knowledge of spiritual reality and is concerned with the highest vibrations of energy which is within the comprehension of man in his present state of being which is much limited by the physical conditions in which he lives. He is too much concerned with matter and a material universe to be able to look beyond to the great spiritual cosmos which is the creative force behind the material appearance he regards as the only reality. The material world is but a mirage or reverse of the spiritual.

Some further questions and answers were as follows:

Qn. As ectoplasm is affected by light, can ectoplasm affect weak light?

Ans. Yes.

Qn. If this is correct, could ectoplasm be used to modulate light falling onto a photo-electric cell and so produce speech?

Ans. When electrical processes are used we are able to manifest more easily because it is another way in which we can bring our vibration nearer to the level of the physical world so that both speech and materialisation can be brought into recognisable manifestation. It is, therefore, possible to use ectoplasm to modulate light in the way you suggest.

On the 13th February 1962, the following communication was received in the same way:

I am William Crookes and I have a special message to send to the group of men who are trying to get scientific information which will enable them to make contact with the world usually called the next world. As a matter of fact, it is not a world which is in any sense of the word a distant world or a future world for those still on the earth plane, but a 'now' world. You are in one sense living in it now. Your real self, which is not visible, being hidden in its apparently fleshy exterior, is in close contact with that part of the world which is still unseen. What we are trying to do is to bring into focus this world now invisible to you. The way this can and will be done is by a combination of processes in which the physical and metaphysical will meet. In order to achieve this, it must be realised that mental as well as physical processes must be used. The mind of man is a much more powerful instrument than is commonly recognised and it must be utilised in the same way, tho' in a lesser degree, that we use it on this other plane of life. We do not and cannot utilise the physical processes since we are no longer concerned with measurements, tho' we, of course, realise that the scientists on your side are still using measurement as a gauge on which to base their thesis on all their experiments with atomic energy. We are deeply troubled about the wrong uses to which the recent knowledge gained has been put. It must be known that man has achieved knowledge of forces which, without spiritual advancement, can do more than destroy his achievements of the past by destroying his whole inheritance as the sons of God. I mean it is a moral issue and will be a tragedy of the whole venture of earthly existence if this new knowledge is put to destructive rather than constructive uses. I therefore exhort all who have seen the red light to turn their thoughts towards the acquirement of spiritual knowledge. Then the way will be shown and contact will be achieved. To this end, the study of metaphysics is all important and with it the prayer and faith through which comes the knowledge and wisdom to use that knowledge. Then the secrets will be revealed — the secrets which, to us, are open secrets of life and the universe.

William Crookes.

A further set of questions were sent to Miss Rosher on the 6th April 1962 as follows:

Qn. With reference to your communication in February 1962 and your statement that the way in which your world will be brought into focus will be a combination of processes in which the physical and metaphysical will meet, can the phenomena we know as Radionics be used to bridge the gap between physics and metaphysics?

Ans. It is possible.

Qn. If Radionics is considered suitable, is faith in the equipment of principle importance?

Ans. Not necessarily.

Qn. In order to help to bridge the gap by using the mind, should one develop the mind on psychic lines?

Ans. Yes.

Qn. If so, can you suggest any means by which such development could be accelerated?

Ans. When making your preparations for developing your psychic gifts do so in an atmosphere of spiritual attention so that you can receive the thought impressions transferred to you from this side by those of us who are seeking to guide your researches.

William Crookes.

As we were intrigued at receiving these communications which purported to be written by Sir William Crookes, we wrote to the British Museum and obtained a photostat copy of a letter written on the 21st January 1873 and signed, "William Crookes".

I then forwarded the following documents to an amateur, but highly recommended graphologist:

A. Part of a letter written by Miss Rosher to me.

B. The communication by Sir William Crookes dated 30th January 1961.

C. Part of the photostat copy of the letter written by Sir William Crookes on the 21st January 1873.

The graphologist's report on sample B read:

> This is very interesting in that it does not reveal a normal self-conscious identity. It begins normally, then there is a loss of identity after a moment of deliberation. The writer then appears to have become a development of a consistent nervous, disembodied energy, with a slight suggestion of deliberation and will power coming to the surface only occasionally. Physically there is a suggestion of considerable age and an experienced acceptance of the inevitable. The whole gives the impression of impersonal, negative spirituality.

I had been careful to write to the graphologist as an individual, with no reference to our Society. In view of this, we found the report very interesting.

His comparison of sample B with sample C was not conclusive. It read:

> B lacks all the creative originality and personal idiosyncracies of C and, if there could be any association, it is in the capacity for mental drive. B is then the impersonalised, physically aged, reflection of either (or both) A and C.

Having met Miss Rosher on several occasions, in addition to receiving long letters from her, I am aware that the communications which she has received, not only from Gordon Burdick, but also her father, mother and other relatives, have brought her and those she has been able to help much happiness and a deeper understanding of life.

At the end of her book she writes:

> In conclusion, I have to admit, that in carrying out the constantly expressed wish of my communicator, Gordon Burdick, all that he had told me of what he called "the other side of life" should be made public, since he had been required to give this information to a world in need; that it was work that God had given him to do, I was at first reluctant to obey. My own natural inclination was to keep the information to myself and a few intimates. This had not been permitted and, in carrying out this duty placed upon me by one to whom I could not find it in my heart to say "No", I sincerely hope that those who have read the foregoing pages have felt their faith strengthened.

And their hearts comforted and assured that life goes on and that our loved ones are not far off, but very close at hand, helping those of us who are left behind to continue the struggle in a world of conflicts.

To me, this is a splendid example of God working through people, both in this world and the world of spirit.

In 1965, I received a letter from Miss Rosher dated the 30th January which was the day on which the state funeral of Sir Winston Churchill was held. He had died on the 24th January. In this letter she wrote:

> We watched the funeral of Winston Churchill on T.V. There has never I feel been a state funeral quite like it, or to equal it, but what one felt all through was that this was not an occasion for mourning or sorrow in the ordinary sense but rather a farewell to one who was departing the earthly scene after an inspiring and triumphant life or pilgrimage, *not ended* but moving forward to even greater achievements. On the 19th of last month, I had a communication from Gordon in which he said, "You know that Winston Churchill is expected over here. I just want to tell you that great preparations are being made to receive him". There was more to it than that and he finished up by saying he would have more to tell me in a little while. However, I heard nothing more until the evening of the 24th when he wrote, "We are waiting to hear when Churchill will be ready to be received by the great assembly gathering to welcome him. He is at present resting quietly in the place prepared for him." He also said, "You will be feeling a sense of loss, the loss of the grand old warrior. We will be gaining a young and great and vigorous helper in the work to be done so your loss is our gain in this world." I feel I am very fortunate to be getting, unasked, dispatches from "The other side".

In October 1965, when speaking at a public meeting at Reading, Miss Rosher told us of a communication on the 2nd February which said that Churchill had been given a tremendous welcome. He had been placed on a dais and former prime ministers of Great Britain, great soldiers and sailors and famous men of the past had paid him homage.

VII

DR. CHARLES MARSHALL AND JOCK

On several occasions, I visited the London medium, Leslie Flint, with a small group of friends from Newbury when spirit communications were recorded on tape.

One of the spirit communicators in 1955 claimed to be a Dr. Charles Marshall. He was a fluent communicator who gave talks and answered questions. None of the group knew Dr. Marshall and we wondered why he had contacted us.

One evening, a member of the group telephoned me to say that he had found a reference to a Dr. Charles Marshall in Hannen Swaffer's book, *My Greatest Story*. This excited our interest so I wrote to Hannen Swaffer, telling him of our experiences and asking if it was possible to contact any near relatives of Dr. Marshall. I received a reply telling me that Dr. Marshall's widow, Mrs. Blanche Marshall, lived at Leigh-on-Sea, Essex and giving her address.

I then wrote to Mrs. Marshall, relating our experiences, and asking her if she would like to meet us in London and hear the tape recording. Mrs. Marshall replied that she would be delighted to meet us in London and hear the recording. She said that her husband had spoken to her through Leslie Flint about ten years previously.

Arrangements were made and another member of the group and I met Mrs. Marshall in London and she heard the tape recording. She confirmed that, although the tone of the voice was not exactly similar to that of her husband, the phrases used and the manner of speaking could be easily recognised.

We then arranged to meet Mrs. Marshall again to join us in another seance with Leslie Flint. Once again the proceedings were recorded on tape and we found the reunion of Dr. and Mrs. Marshall very impressive. The following extract from the recording is of interest but it is impossible to convey the tones and feelings expressed:

Dr. M. Hello, hello, I'm so pleased to come — it's Peter.

Mrs. M. God Bless you, Peter.

Dr. M. Hello, dear. God bless you. Gosh! I'm so pleased that you have come. I've been praying and looking forward to this. Mr. S. and your friends, I am so grateful to you for bringing my wife. It is kind of you! I've been hoping and praying that it would be possible to talk to you like this. Of course, I do get other opportunities, I know, but to talk in this fashion is, well, what I've been looking forward to so much and for so long.

Well, dear, I don't have to ask you how you are because I know. I'm with you constantly, you know that only too well.

Mrs. M. Yes, I do. You get my thoughts and I get yours.

Dr. M. I do, every day, every day I come to you. Not a day passes that I don't come to you. You know that. And then we have our little talks through the instrument.

Mrs. M. Yes, yes.

Dr. M. Which I look forward to, of course, very much indeed. And our work is going on. I'm very, very pleased with it.

Mrs. M. You are pleased with the patients?

Dr. M. Yes, I am. We've made some very good progress, especially with some. Of course, there are bound to be some that we can't do much for.

We were very surprised to hear Dr. Marshall announce himself as "Peter" as he had always given his name to us as Dr. Charles Marshall. However, this was explained when I received the following comment in a letter which Mrs. Marshall wrote to me on the 14th June 1956:

Dr. Marshall was always known as "Peter" by his family and close friends — a name I gave him many years ago and is linked with Peter Pan and Sir James Barrie (who has spoken with me several times), in fact we were linked in fantasy — Peter, Wendy and our sons were Michael and John. I possess many links connected with this famous play, including friendship of the players at that time over 40 years ago. The music was written by a friend of ours, Johnny Crook, now passed over. It has been said that, when I pass over, I will hear the lovely setting for "The arrival of Wendy"! John is in spirit with his father. Michael, on earth, has a little son also called "Peter Marshall". I am called Wendy by my close friends.

We found that Dr. Marshall had been particularly interested in the treatment of cancer and that Mrs. Marshall was continuing his work. The following report was written by Kay Ryde and published in the weekly newspaper, *Psychic News* dated the 6th September 1958:

Some time ago, I was at a direct voice seance, when a Dr. Marshall came through from spirit and spoke to me. He talked about healing and what he said impressed me to contact his wife on earth although she was a stranger to me at the time.

Mrs. Blanche Marshall and I, therefore, met and we were both astonished when we found in conversation that we had an amazing link. My aunt was well known to her and had lived in the same house at Hampstead as she and Dr. Marshall.

When Dr. Charles Marshall, M.D., M.Sc., F.R.C.S., was on earth, he was a keen believer in spirit contact and spirit healing; he and Mrs. Marshall sat together in meditation and received automatic writings which convinced him that cancer could be cured by means of spiritual healing and an injection, of which he was given the formula.

He wrote a book on the subject but, because the treatment was unorthodox, it was not accepted by the medical fraternity.

Undaunted, Dr. Marshall sacrificed his career by his pursuit of the subject, and impoverished himself in so doing. Then pneumonia attacked him and he died. This was a dreadful blow to Mrs. Marshall for they were a devoted couple but, when the shock passed, spirit messages convinced her that Dr. Marshall wanted her to carry on his work with his guidance from his new life and experience.

This she has done faithfully despite advancing years, a very small income and a tiny home. The injection formula has been improved and is called Marshelium and this is used, plus spiritual healing. Any cases of cancer have been treated after doctors have pronounced the patient beyond medical skill and doomed to die.

Mrs. Marshall now lives on the coast and was guided by her husband to contact a practising doctor there who now believes in the work. When hospitals and medicine can do little more for his cancer patients, he hands them over to Mrs. Marshall. The results in many cases have surprised him!

Two years ago, a doctor contacted her with a woman who was discharged from a London hospital with incurable cancer of the spine and breast. Mrs. Marshall took over and the Marshelium was used in conjunction with loving and devoted spiritual healing.

The woman recovered and the doctor sent her back to the hospital two years after she was doomed to die, for extensive examination. The surgeon reported, "No secondaries of cancer in the breast cavity. No secondaries of cancer in spinal area. Blood tests quite satisfactory. Physical exercises normal."

This is a wonderful thing. The doctor was most impressed although of course professional etiquette does not allow him to disclose his name or case file.

Eminent doctors abroad have heard of the treatment and are more than interested. Now a doctor trained in Edinburgh and living in South Africa is anxious to use the preparation and the spiritual healing (the two must go together).

When funds allow, Mrs. Marshall hopes to be able to go overseas to them and help them in their work. Although most cases do not come to Mrs. Marshall until medical treatment has failed, she stresses that the earlier the treatment can be given, the better chance there is of recovery.

Mrs. Marshall has had to fight prejudices, antagonism and exploitation. Her home does not permit her to have a sanctuary there but, nothing daunted, this valiant little woman travels to her patient's homes.

All she asks is co-operation, patience and faith. She cannot promise a cure, this does not rest with her, but if the patient opens his or her mind and soul to the healing power, then benefit of some sort is bound to be felt.

Congratulations Dr. and Mrs. Marshall — and the doctor

who is brave enough to co-operate with their work for the suffering and desperate!

Having met Mrs. Marshall on several occasions, corresponded with her for some years and received details of successful treatments of cancer cases, I consider that Kay Ryde wrote a very fair report. I held great respect and admiration for Mrs. Marshall's faith and courage in her uphill battle.

The following paragraphs have been extracted from communications received from Dr. Marshall during seances held with Leslie Flint in London:

One must always bear in mind that nature takes its course in so many different ways that, eventually, with all the healing, with all the cures, the time must come when people have to leave behind the physical body. I mean, in the very advanced cases, it is very difficult to do very much for them. One can alleviate pain but you cannot necessarily bring about a cure if it has got to such a stage, such an advanced stage in the system that there is very little hope of a cure. Then, of course, nature must take its course.

I think the basis, the fundamental thing is right thinking and right living which should start from childhood. I think, of course, there's no doubt about it, these things are hereditary, they are passed on from parents to children and perhaps from generation, two or three generations back. It may sound unjust. Some people say it is a bad thing as it doesn't seem to indicate a God of love. These things are sort of pulled from one generation to another but one must always remember that our bodies are physical beings, they are material things, they are composed of the elements of the earth. These things do pass from one to another and, until we get a generation ahead when people perhaps can be trained to think on the right lines and live on the right lines, we shall always be trying to eradicate illness and disease until such times in generations perhaps hence people will think and act differently and be trained.

That is why, the whole point of their coming back to earth is to make people realise the responsibilities they have to each other and to themselves and the future generations. When this is a truth that is accepted by all nations, we shall eventually break down all these barriers, creeds and dogmas and have one universal religion of love and tolerance and understanding and of communion with our world.

When people realise that all worlds are one, that we are all linked together in brotherhood and that we are all part of God Himself, when people get the right angle and aspect of these things, they will think and act differently, then they will have healthy bodies.

That's the thing we've got to aim at, that's the fundamental thing behind all that we are trying to do. We try to patch up, we try to cure, we are trying to help people, of course we are from this side through doctors, through healers, through mediums, through every source that is available to us but the fundamental thing is that we've got to go further than that. We've got to go into the many years that lie ahead when we shall hope for new generations of people yet unborn who will be able to think and act differently and will live in tranquility and peace and harmony among themselves and with other nations when men and women everywhere will be of one spirit. That's what we've got to aim for.

When this is an accepted fact and people realise that there is no such thing as death, that life is eternal and that communion is a fact between the two worlds, when all these things are realities in their minds, then there will be a different race of men. That's what we are all working and aiming for. You all realise that, of course.

And in answer to a question on healing, Dr. Marshall said:

One must remember this, in healing it is not necessary always to lay on hands. There are people who are natural healers. There are some who have no need to be in a position to go into trance or make passes. There is such a thing as magnetic healing . . .

The water is, in itself, very helpful, especially in certain instances. It absorbs. This is very difficult to explain and more difficult for you to follow, but it definitely absorbs a substance which is taken from the body of a sick person. If we, as we do, when giving our treatment, take from the individual concerned certain matters which are not visible to the eye, the water is useful because it can absorb. That is why it should, when you start, be fresh and pure from running water and immediately afterwards it should be dispensed with. It may not make sense to you.

I don't know how one can explain certain things as we are working with rays, working with conditions which are far beyond your knowledge and experience and I must say this, although it may sound strange to you, that, lately, we have had more difficulty, though it is not anyone's fault; but we have had difficulty with conditions around the earth. They are very bad. The disturbance in the ether. This atomic energy which has been released is doing a great deal of harm. You may not see any reaction of it at the moment but, probably in a few month's time you will. I think there will be some mysterious illnesses. The tragedy of it is that, unless something is done about this atomic energy, this power that is being released, the gamma rays and so on, they are going to do tremendous harm which may not show up immediately but, eventually, I think there is going to be a great deal of trouble in certain directions — especially in certain places . . .

The point is, if they are honest with themselves, and I'm afraid it's very difficult for a scientist to be honest with himself for the simple reason that he doesn't know himself what is being achieved or what can be achieved. But he has an idea, he assumes the proof can only be had after the experiments have taken place and sometimes, after the experiment has taken place, not only has he done certain things, but, eventually, he realises that a certain harm may have been done of which he had no previous knowledge or realisation. The point is, that here they are dealing with a certain force which is beyond their comprehension at the moment. They don't seem to realise the effect that these rays, they are rays although they don't fully understand perhaps yet exactly what they are, that certain rays, a certain power is released which is definitely harmful to the human body. We can see and we can appreciate the reaction it is going to have on human beings and on animal life. It is going to affect the bone structure of the physical body. I think you're going to have a lot more of, what you might term, paralysis or polio. There are other things it can do.

In answer to a question about absent healing, he said:

Let me explain this business quite clearly if I can. I'll only explain my own angle — I don't profess to explain other people's. For instance, you know a lot of people go to seances and they request the guide to get in touch with John Jones who died in 1913. Now, how the devil could one of any intelligence expect us to go paging the heavens to find a particular person who died in 1913 or whenever it was any more than you could expect us to come to you to find someone who may be living you don't even know where. There might be thousands of people with the same name. It isn't easy. But, when you know the person, there is a link and we can work on that link, on the vibration, there is something tangible to work on. But, these odd "bods", as it were, whom you link up with, whom we don't know and you don't know, it does present a task. All we can do is to mentally concentrate a spiritual force upon their name, hoping that it will reach the person concerned.

You must never credit us with powers which we don't pretend to have. We don't pretend to be omnipotent and we don't know everything. We don't know all the answers. There are a lot of things we would like to know, we don't know. There are a lot of things we would like to be able to do, we can't do. We strive to do things we're not sure we can do for it is very complex but, the point is, one must bear in mind this, that the power of thought is tremendous and you can prove that for yourselves in various ways. No doubt, you've already done that and it is nothing to do with Spiritualism as such or psychic matters as such. You've only got to get two people who are in tune mentally and have much in common, they often pick up each other's thoughts and know exactly what the person has been thinking about a split second afterwards and so on. You've all had those kind of experiences, I suppose, some time or another.The point is that there's so much that can be done by mind, the power of mind is tremendous. For instance, we come to you, we transmit our thoughts to you. Sometimes you pick them up, sometimes you don't. For instance, I come and speak to you here. You hear a voice. It's probably a voice that's distinctive. You recognise it again. You don't know what the person looks like behind the voice but you know the voice as such. The point is that what you hear is not really, in a sense, a voice at all. It is really a transmission of my thoughts into sound via the voice-box which is built up from ectoplasm. It is, in a sense, artificial but, according to the person behind it and according to the person's personality, according to the person's power of being able to, sort of, push over or transmit their personality and thought to some degree, they can make the voice-box respond and it can become to your ears a fairly well distinct voice and if you have known the person previously, you might say, "Oh, it's a very good reproduction — it sounds like him." But, often, you must remember that, when your relations come, inexperienced, perhaps emotional, over-excited, you get so many things that they have to contend with. The voice-box can only respond to what they are able to give over. In consequence, you may get a hotch-potch — some of it not sounding perhaps like the voice of the person, some of it giving the things which are intentional, some things which are confusing. You ask them questions, making them even more confused. There are many factors which you must take into consideration with all communications, particularly anything that comes into this line of thought where we are transmitting into sound via an artificial voice-box. Your thoughts enter into it and intermingle and confuse. The medium's, particularly if he is agitated or over anxious or worried. There's so much we ought to tell you about communication which I hope some of us may be able to do eventually. It would not only help you but it would help a lot of people who you are trying to interest in this subject. It is very important. The point is this, as I am trying to explain to you, a lot of work which is done from your point of view is done by thought process. It is you that send out your thoughts. In other words, you send out your prayers that they might be helpful to the people concerned and you look to us to try to help and to do what we can. Well, we do what we can under the given circumstances but you must remember there is a limit to what we can do and, according to the links that are made. If they are strong links we can do a great deal, if the links are weak we can do very little.

The following report was published in *Psychic News* dated the 11th July 1964:

Intervention by a spirit doctor saved the life of Mrs. Pauline Liberman when she was given only two hours to live. She had an emergency operation for a septic kidney with a stone in it.

During it she "saw" a group of white-robed figures standing around something. There was one man taller than the rest, but she could not see their faces.

Mrs. Liberman, of Sherwood Road, London, N.W.4. told no-one of her experience. Six months later she sat with direct voice medium Leslie Flint. The medium knew his sitter but was unaware that she had even been in hospital.

During the seance a voice addressed Mrs. Liberman saying: "I am Dr. Marshall. It was not a dream, I was taking over from the earthly doctors. The other figures were your dear ones standing around you."

She then realised that she had been out of her body and the group she had seen were standing around her. She had never heard of Dr. Marshall when she called at *Psychic News* to tell her story.

We were able to tell her that the man who saved her life was Dr. C. F. Marshall. He was a Spiritualist who in a spirit message was given a cancer cure which he used effectively on some "incurable" patients. But medical colleagues did not pay attention to the results. Later a South African doctor took up the cure and also announced that it had cured cancer.

Marshall has spoken through Flint's mediumship before. The doctor's widow listened to a tape-recording of his return at one direct-voice seance, and asserted, "It was my husband's voice." She also commented on the many typical phrases that he used.

How effective was the healing? Mrs. Liberman told *Psychic News* that when she left hospital an eminent surgeon told her, "You are one of our miracles." Much later she had an X-ray to determine her present condition. The doctor commented that he had never seen a kidney in such a good condition in a patient who had suffered from one that was septic.

A fairly frequent spirit communicator to our group in Newbury was someone who spoke with a Scotch accent whom we called Jock. It was very interesting, therefore, to visit Leslie

Flint in London and have further talks with the same communicator but using a different medium. The following extracts from his communications are included because of their general interest:

Jock: If you get the results that we're aiming at and you build it up and strengthen it over a period of time then, gradually, we'll ask you to invite people who need help and comfort so that you can do some work. Because it would not be right to keep it to yourselves.
Sitter: We don't intend to. I thought you might have something over and above that — other than just covering ordinary people coming for consolation.
Jock: Aye, but that's important and one must remember that. But, who knows, if we make the progress that we may make then perhaps we'll be able to do something in a scientific way that will help to bring conviction to those damn hard-headed people . . .

The whole thing is so delicate and so sensitive that you've only got to have one person there who is antagonistic or who has a wrong vibration and he can upset all the things we are doing and they can probably put the circle back for weeks or months. You see, it is dangerous to ask the wrong people because, in their experiments if they're so-called scientific, they will want to introduce some kind of scientific instruments to prove things that might have a detrimental effect upon the whole thing. You see, the point is, you cannot take years to build something up which is so sensitive that you cannot even describe it. I mean, after all is said and done, a medium is a very sensitive person and the point is that, if we were experimenting and someone were to do something silly, it could be very dangerous and could do a great deal of harm . . .

Perhaps I don't call things sinful that you might, or at least, have been led to believe is sinful. That's the difference. You have to abide by the rules of society and I think that some of the rules are damn silly. What comes naturally is not necessarily sinful. A lot of the people who have made the rules are pretty good sinners themselves. In any case, I don't think there is much point in us pursuing that. After all, I I shall get told off for coming down and not elevating you a

bit. I don't want to get in the bad books of the "higher ups".
Sitter: Can you tell us anything about the "higher ups", Jock, or aren't you allowed to?
Jock: Aye, I can tell you plenty about the "higher ups". There's all kinds from all kinds of spheres and stratas according to their enlightenment and development and I don't profess, myself, to be anything like the wonderful people I have met. Maybe, eventually, I will, but it's a slow process. No-one suddenly becomes highly elevated. It takes a long time and when I talk about time it's difficult to explain because our time isn't like yours. At the same time, you learn gradually that you cannot assimilate knowledge and experience at once, not even over here. You don't suddenly become perfect like some people in your world like to think. You know, it amuses me when some people have the idea that because they've been so-called living a good life and going to church regularly and all the rest of it like a kind of life insurance when they come here they're alright. They've got a big mistake coming to them. Some of those people think they can buy their way to heaven. You cannot buy your way by bowing the knee and going to church and giving a few pence for the new organ and all that. That's not the way. The way to find your way here and gain knowledge and experience and make real progress is when you sacrifice yourself for others and forget self in service. It doesn't matter what you call your creed or religion, it's how you live that counts. Anyway, I know that much with experience but some of the souls here are great and wonderful souls and they are a great help and encouragement to many of us who are not so progressed. One day when you make more progress you'll find you will be getting contacts with some wonderful people but, you know, its like everything else, you've got to be patient and take time and build up to that gradually.
Sitter: When you are not working with the circles, Jock, what do you do with your time?
Jock: Well, the best part of the time is, what I call, rescue work, helping the souls who are earthbound or in need. I was doing quite a lot of that just after the war on the battlefields and places where people were still clinging to the old ideas of things, you know, they could not break their minds

from the old associations and it was our task to try and help them to see and to visualise and to realise the new existence that was waiting for them once they got away from earth.

Sitter: What would you say the majority of people do?

Jock: You mean over here? You mean immediately after death — the average person?

Sitter: Yes.

Jock: Well, the average person, on passing out, usually finds himself met by relations and friends who have gone on before and they're brought to an environment which is, in some ways, not unlike earth. That is, if you can visualise earth without all the snags. Here, we have magnificent countryside with beautiful flowers and birds and pets and animals just the same as you do on earth. We have every type of scenery imaginable I should think and we have lovely little places where people can rest in and relax and gradually become aware of their new conditions. Surroundings become, as it were, part of their new life and their friends and relations help them gradually and open their eyes and take them around and so on. Everything is a gradual state of process and of progress. It's very like your earth in many ways.

Sitter: And do you read?

Jock: Sure, you've got plenty of books here. You can have books galore. Over here you can have every book that's ever been written and you know, another thing here, once you begin to realise and learn, you begin to realise that languages are no barriers any more and you begin to read, and I'm not talking only of books, but I'm talking about people. You can realise when you see a person what they are really like for their true selves, not like you do on earth — sometimes you get deceived. Here, no-one can hide their true self from another and you are able, too, to read all the thoughts that they are trying to send out. In fact, after a time, you realise it is not essential to vibrate the atmosphere and create sound and make a voice. You can communicate almost entirely by thought process. In a sense you do that on earth but you have to vibrate the atmosphere to make sound otherwise people get your thoughts via that but here you can, if you wish, after a time, dispense with that. Although, actually of course, there are many people here who still like to talk and they do, and there's many a person here who likes to sing and they do sing. When you first come here you carry over the old ideas of eating and drinking and you do those things automatically. They are there for you if you want them. But, after a time, you realise that those things aren't essential and, as you lose the desire for things so they disappear.

Sitter: And, when a Chinese goes over or somebody from here, they tend to go to a section where most of their own nationality are, I suppose?

Jock: At first, but what you've got to remember is that here we don't recognise nationalities or different creeds — you know that. But, over here, it would be natural for a Chinese for instance, to go to his family and to his friends. But, gradually, he would begin to realise that there was a great outer world among peoples with whom he would mingle and mix until he'd lose his nationality as such. He'd no longer be considered, shall we say, as a Chinese or a Hindu, he'd be considered one of the great human race and all the traits and all the peculiarities associated with a particular national way of thought would gradually disappear as he assimilated his new existence and life. One of the first things you are taught when you come here is to realise that, here, you are all part of the one God, you are all part of the one Father, and, in consequence, you gradually lose a lot of the old ideas about race and creed and all that. As a matter of fact, the first things you have to learn here are the things which often aren't considered most important on earth. You see, if people on earth would forget that they are of this nation or that nation or that that nation is greater than the other, forget all the things that make up for hatred and malice and intolerance and breed wars. That's the trouble, you've got too many dividing barriers. If you could make the world one place, and all people one people, that's the beginning of the great things which we hope, one day, to accomplish. That's one of the reasons why we come down to you, of course, to try and break down all the silly barriers that man has built up in his ignorance and his foolishness. To get something more like a universal understanding of what mankind really is — part of the great Universe. You see, the trouble with the world and why you have wars and all the rest of it is because of nations and all the dividing things that you have in your world.

In answer to a question about royalty passing to the spirit world, Jock said:

In the old days, when the people like kings and queens had very great power and they had great homage paid to them, those people found it more difficult and gradually had to change their outlook but not so much now. Modern kings and queens who are much more democratic, much more part of the people and who really carry a heavy burden which probably, if they had had their way, they wouldn't have wanted. For instance, when King George V and VI, both the Georges and Queen Mary and people like that came here they soon settled down to a completely new way of life and it didn't worry them that people were not bowing and scraping. I think, too, in many ways, they led very good lives in trying to sacrifice themselves for the good of their people, I think, more than people realise. And those people are only too glad to be able to settle down to a quiet, happy existence without pomp and ceremony.

Sitter: Do you choose what you do or are you, sort of, detailed?

Jock: Well, most people, I think I can go as far as to say, all people more or less choose what they would like to do but there are exceptional cases where people are requested to do a certain type of work and it is very rare for anyone to refuse because they know that it is for their own good, too. You know, it is an extraordinary thing here, we realise not that we do a thing because we want to get something out of it because that's the last thought in our minds but, when we're helping others, we invariably help ourselves for we all live by and learn by and from each other. I mean, even by coming down to you, in a sense, I learn something from you. You might not think that's feasible but it's true. I can assure you that, often, I learn things by coming back to earth and meeting earthly people and going around and keeping my eyes open and I realise that people can teach me something whether they're on your sphere or on my own or on a higher sphere. In other words, one's always assimilating knowledge and experience and we're all living and learning and breathing, you might say, by each other. And, of course, that is life! No man can live to himself .That's the trouble with some of these people who think they are so high and mighty. The first thing they have to unlearn is that they're not. A man is only high and mighty in the true sense when he's most humble.

VIII

WHOLENESS AND HOLINESS

When one recognizes that man is a spiritual being temporarily inhabiting a physical body so that he may undergo experiences which are necessary for his spiritual evolution, many anomalies in the average man's attitude to life become apparent. One of these is the general approach to health.

It seems to me that the increasing incidence of illness and a situation with doctors overworked, hospitals full, with long waiting lists for operations and with steady increase in the amount of drugs issued is a terrible indictment of civilisation in the 1970's.

It does not appear to be the policy of the Ministry of Social Services to treat man as a whole — as a trinity of body, mind and spirit which must all be functioning in harmony for health and wholeness. There is a tendency to limit man into two of the three functions so that doctors deal with the physical body and psychologists and psychiatrists deal with the mind. As psychosomatic illness is now recognised, the relationship between the mind and body is becoming clearer but the need for complete harmony between body, mind and spirit is still not fully recognised, although it is now admitted that a broken heart can be a cause of death.

If one gives further consideration to man as a trinity, it is clear that he lives under a system of physical laws, mental laws and spiritual laws and that, if he breaks any of these, he creates a disharmony which automatically results in disease.

At the physical level it is easy to understand that the body needs a balanced diet, fresh air and exercise, and more and more people are becoming aware that our faulty diet is the cause of much illness. We have lost the concept of the dignity of man as a spiritual being and the physical body as the temple of the soul.

In a foreword to a booklet issued by The Soil Association which contains a lecture given by Dr. Aubrey T. Westlake, B.M.B. B.Chir (Cantab) M.R.C.S. L.R.C.P. in 1964 one reads:

> Man's wasteful and greedy exploitation of the earth's natural resources and his contamination of his environment is as old as history but the speed has accelerated alarmingly in our own generation. The very survival of the human race depends upon recognising this and accepting the challenge. The degeneration of health through reliance upon processed foods, new drugs, chemically sprayed food: the menace of atomic wastes and radio activity resulting from atomic explosions: the pollution of air and water which passes through the human organism, all this constitutes a threat to life.

I was very interested to meet Dr. Westlake when he spoke at a meeting organised by our society at Aldermaston.

It is extraordinary to me that housewives will accept the massive barrage of advertising material put out by food manufacturers rather than investigate the claim that the food sold in Health Food Stores is purer than most other foods: It is obvious that the quality of the food we eat affects the quality of our bodies and it is astonishing that this simple statement of fact is not more widely recognised. Those concerned with racehorses or dog racing take great care with the feeding of the animals, but do not always apply the same care to their own bodies. Young mothers who have children suffering from dental decay at an early age are generally not aware that the European Committee of the World Health Organisation has stated that the main causes of dental decay are the foods and sweets made from white flour and white sugar.

I have heard a doctor of medicine describe an experiment in which two sets of rabbits were fed on two identical beds of cabbages. The soil in one bed had been treated with compost and the soil in the other with artificial fertilisers. The set of rabbits which were fed on the cabbages grown on soil treated with artificial fertilisers became ill.

More and more people are becoming concerned with the quality of food and the difficulty of obtaining wholesome food. In my opinion, the use of chemicals has been extended beyond reasonable care and the question of the quality of foods has not been given sufficient emphasis. We need to regain the concept of the dignity of man as a spiritual being. Everything else will then be approached in the right way.

I introduced Health Foods into a shop at Newbury and they have been sold regularly ever since. I also joined the Reading Vegetarian and Food Reform Society and the Soil Association which is another minority group which is concerned with maintaining the natural balance of the soil. Thoughtful people must be aware that the fact that such groups exist indicates that there is something wrong with our society and those responsible for feeding the nation.

Few people realize the power of thought and that there can be a direct relationship between wrong thinking and physical illness. One wonders how many church members really appreciate the meaning of the part of the Confession when they say, "We have offended against thy Holy laws!" Negative thoughts and emotions can cause physical illness. But the whole of the Christian teaching is positive. Jesus said, "Have courage! Be of good cheer!"

When I served in the army, I knew a man whose reactions to mental pressure resulted in a rash appearing on his forehead and neck. Also, when I worked in the Post Office, I remember the case of a lady clerk who always developed migraine when the quarterly balance of accounts was due.

I have a list of 44 physical complaints which, according to one authority, can be due to certain mental attitudes. Some of these are:

Asthma	—	Anxiety.
Stiff Back	—	Hurt feelings.
High Blood Pressure	—	Anger, long-continued vexations and strain.
Kidney Troubles	—	Narrowness and fixity of the mind; bitter feelings.
Knee Trouble	—	Indecision (weak at the knees).
Liver Trouble	—	Criticism, resentment, prejudice, ill-humour.
Rheumatism:		
Muscular Fibrositis	—	Smothered or suppressed resentment.

Rheumatoid Arthritis	—	Denied emotional energy.
Osteo-arthritis	—	Self-willed, agressive and self-opiniated states.
Shoulder and Neck Ache	—	Too intense sense of responsibility.
Sleeplessness	—	Insecurity.

As a result of experience in Psychical Research, one gradually gains a new concept of man and, therefore, of oneself. One begins to appreciate the great power of the mind in determining the quality of our lives. One realizes that every word we speak, every action we take originate in the mind. One begins to appreciate that, although the mind functions through the physical brain and can function separately from the brain, it is also a tool, like a computer, to be used wisely by the thinker. Once this concept has been reached, it is possible to control thought by recognising thoughts before they become effective in words or actions and to transmute them into positive thoughts which are constructive and helpful. *If one can accomplish this, it can be a "turning point" in one's life as one will be living more in harmony with the basic purpose in life — spiritual progress.* Negative thoughts and emotions are barriers to progress.

When religious people use the phrase "Thy Will be done", they infer the existence of Divine Laws. I have no doubt at all that there are Divine or Eternal Laws upholding all creation including man and that, if we wish to be healthy, we dare not ignore these spiritual laws. There can be a sickness of the soul which automatically results in detrimental effects in the mind and physical body. A person whose spirit is free and adventurous will often express this in their face and in free and natural body movements — walking, bending, etc. A person whose spirit is cramped by strong negative emotions such as fear will often express this physically in their face and by their lack of ease and grace in physical movements. The phrase, "As within, so without" appears to apply in such cases. In the same way, but much more important, as the physical body requires the right food and regular exercise, the spirit also requires spiritual "food" and spiritual exercise. This should be obtained by the adoption of daily habits of prayer and meditation, by giving a loving service to others wherever possible and by gaining spiritual strength by joining others in corporate praise and worship. It is this inner strength which can overcome any problems which may beset us in this earthly life. Because of this basic inner need of man, one can understand why churches were built throughout the land so that the opportunities for corporate worship were available. It is sad, however, that the living spirit of the early Church appears to have been confined by the intellectual approach in our theological colleges. This has resulted in a failure to communicate the real vitality of the Christian message which has naturally been followed by a decline in church attendance. In these circumstances, it is not surprising that many people seek their "Wholeness" by joining small groups for meditation which is often based on Eastern teachings.

IX

SPIRIT POSSESSION AND OBSESSION

When Air Marshal Lord Dowding spoke to members of our Society at Aldermaston, he mentioned that, in his opinion, 10% of the cases in mental homes were cases of possession by ignorant spirits and, if they were treated as such, they could probably be released.

Dr. Raynor C. Johnson of Melbourne University stated in one of his letters to me that he thought the ratio of such cases was two in five.

I had been aware for some years of the work of Dr. Carl Wickland, M.D., member of the Chicago Medical Society, the Illinois State Medical Society and the American Association for the advancement of Science. Dr. Wickland carried out research into cases of possession for thirty years with the help of his wife who had a natural psychic ability.

His method was to use static electricity to dislodge the possessing entity who then entranced his wife. Dr. Wickland was then able to talk to the spirits and explain that they were, so called, 'dead' and link them up with relatives or others in the spirit world who could help them.

In cases where the possessing spirit was very stubborn, Dr. Wickland would threaten to use a further charge of static electricity which felt, to the spirit, like red hot needles. The spirit would then listen to what Dr. Wickland said and could be helped.

Dr. Wickland recorded his verbatim conversations with possessing spirits in his book, *Thirty Years among the Dead*. This book is generally regarded by experienced Spiritualists as a textbook on this subject.

In 1958, I made the acquaintance of a young man and his wife and in September 1959, the wife sought my help. Her husband suffered with pains in the stomach when he relaxed and normal medical treatment had not cleared the trouble. She wished to contact a spiritual healer so I put her in touch with a friend of mine who was a medium and who practised spiritual healing.

My friend was unsuccessful in this case and came to the conclusion that this was a case of spirit possession. As a result, I had a discussion with the wife of the patient in December 1959 and told her that I was prepared to treat her husband's case as one of spirit possession.

A few days later, I attended a meeting of a small group, which included my friend the medium, a physicist and a solicitor. Much to my surprise, the medium was entranced by a spirit who told me not to interfere. He gave his name as John Barker and it was obvious by his references to the names of the young man and his wife and also to stomach pains that he was the possessing spirit concerned with the case. He was unaware that he was 'dead' and it took several discussions to convince him of this. I believe that I was helped in this case by the young man who had "died" as a result of an explosion in December 1957. The contact with John Barker resulted in an improvement in the patient's health.

Having been able to make tape recordings at the seances, I felt that the recordings were valuable and that, perhaps, they could be used to help some of the unfortunate people who were incarcerated in mental homes because the possibility of possession by ignorant spirits was not recognised by the medical profession. I typed out the records of the seances and sent them to:

The Chairman of the National Association for Mental Health.

The Asst. Superintendent of the Mental Hospital where the young man had been a patient.

A doctor in London with an interest in psychic matters.

A doctor who was also a healer.

An authoress and member of the Society for Psychical Research.

The Chairman of the National Federation of Spiritual Healers.

The Leader of a specialist Healing Group of the Spiritualist Association of Great Britain.

Although I had hoped to arouse interest and action in this country which might help those suffering from possession by ignorant spirits, I made no real headway as the general reaction was polite interest. In November 1960, I obtained the name and address of a Spiritualist M.P. as I considered that the problem might be raised in the House of Commons as a Private Member's Bill. Also in November 1960, I wrote to Dr. Karl Muller, Zurich who, at that time, was the President of the International Spiritualist Federation. He gave me some valuable information in his reply which included the following paragraph:

> The best authority on obsession is Dr. Ignacia Ferreira, Director of the Spiritualist Hospital in Uberaba, Brazil . . . I have no doubt that he would consent to having his books translated into English and published. I think that, in his 25 years practice, he has treated well over 1000 obsession cases.

He also gave me the names of people who might be able to help me in Porto Alegré, Buenos Aires and France.

In an article headed, "Does the Church believe in Evil Spirits?" Mr. Peter Lewis wrote in the *Daily Mail* dated 1st February, 1961:

> The Church of England has, temporarily at least, left out mention of the Devil from the revised catechism that is being drafted.
>
> But, at the prompting of Mr. Arthur Macmillan, the Prime Minister's brother, it is considering drafting a new canon to regulate the use of exorcism for persons "possessed" by evil spirits.
>
> When the Archbishops' Commission on Healing considered exorcism two years ago it recommended that a panel of priests and doctors be set up to examine all suspected cases of possession by evil spirits. But nothing has yet been done.
>
> Such a body might not only help the Church. It could bring objective study to bear on a mysterious and comparable gap in our medical, psychological and spiritual knowledge.

I wrote to Mr. Lewis drawing his attention to the work carried out by Dr. Carl Wickland and pointing out that there seemed to be a need to contact and educate the possessing spirits and not to just "drive them out" as the church's ceremony of exorcism appeared to do.

In January 1961, I obtained a list of names and addresses in Brazil, the Argentine, Japan and the U.S.A. from a spiritual healer named Major T. H. Patterson of Kent. In a letter dated 30th March 1961 he wrote:

> Mary and I have been dealing, for the last five months, with what at first was considered to be a mental case (a woman). She was in a mental home several times. Three doctors told her that she had nothing the matter with her; but she was psychic and caused herself to develop a trance condition. She and her husband, Mary and I, now constitute a small circle and her mediumship is developing rapidly. She is also developing healing. Now here is the interesting point — when she developes trance her husband, who had 19 years in the police force (C.I.D.), informs me that the spirit entities who speak through her are exactly the same as she claimed spoke through her when she was, as the doctors say, a mental case.

On the 11th April 1961, when visiting London, I called at the Brazilian and Argentinian Embassies and made enquiries concerning the treatment of cases of possession by ignorant spirits in their countries but was unable to obtain any useful information.

I also attempted to obtain a copy of a journal *Vos Informativa* through the Mexican Embassy but I was unsuccessful.

As a result of the information received from Dr. Karl Muller of Zurich I received an interesting letter dated 27th April 1961 from Mr. Jose S. Fernandez of Buenos Aires who was described as a retired civil engineer and an author of books on psychics. The following paragraphs are extracted from his letter:

> I see that you have a good general knowledge of cases of obsession caused by ignorant or wicked spirits. Dr. Wickland's book on the subject is a classic and I am in complete agreement with Lord Dowding's opinions as well as with Dr. Raynor Johnson of Melbourne University on the existence of this type of mental case. Percentages vary according to

areas and races. I feel that it is well worth informing orthodox professional men about the possibility of this type of cure.

If you can read Portuguese I thoroughly recommend the work of the great Brazilian psychiatrist, Dr. Ignacia Ferreira. He is dedicated to this kind of cure at his Spiritual Hospital at Uberaba, state of Minas Geraes in Brazil.

In Argentina very little is done as this kind of healing is without the law. That is the reason why so few doctors will touch the subject.

I received another letter from Buenos Aires dated 23rd May 1961 which was written in Spanish. A colleague at work translated it and relevant paragraphs are as follows:

It is true that, in all the mental homes in the world, a great many of the inmates are suffering from a harmful influence of ignorant spirits that which Allan Kardec calls "obsession".

In our country, the Spiritualist Societies care for those sick persons who come seeking relief after medical science has failed. The treatment generally carried out is based on the evoking of the obsessing spirit to indoctrination and moralisation. The ignorant spirit is brought by the guides and, once present and incorporated in a trance medium, its indoctrination is proceeded with. In many cases, this task has to be repeated many times, but it has been found that with patience, love and firmness, these spirits, at first stubborn and immovable, little by little give way, repent, and then leave their victims alone. With this, and the use of magnetic passes, many cases have been improved.

All this is carried out with some fear as our laws, under strong pressure from the Roman Catholic Church, are, in this matter, very antiquated and repress this kind of activity.

Brazil is the place where the cure of obsessions is allowed and is a great success. There are there, a great number of doctors and intellectuals who confront this problem with wonderful success. In Rio de Janeiro, in Sao Paulo and in several important cities of Brazil there are spiritualist hospitals where obsession is cured.

I can tell you that there is a project in our country to create a clinic for these illnesses but the greatest difficulty is to get legal authority for it. With regard to Argentinian doctors, I know some who accept or admit obsession as a reason for disorder but they do not say so publicly.

A further letter from Buenos Aires dated 4th May 1961 confirmed the above statements but with the addition of a reference to reincarnation and quoting revenge in respect of an incident in a previous life as a reason for possession.

The most useful information came from S. Conrado Ferrari, Director of the Hospital Spirita at Porto Alegre. In a letter dated 9th March 1961 he wrote:

In Brazil there are thousands of associations, in whose seats sessions are held and called disobsession which are designed to heal persons who are victims of the actions of perverse spirits or of discarnate entities.

The sessions are held in the presence of 8 to 12 persons, of which 4 or 6 are psychophonic mediums duly prepared and accustomed to this kind of activity, dangerous for those who are not prepared. One of the by-standers, also duly qualified, directs it. They sit around a table and concentrate after a prayer calling for the help of powerful spirits of goodness. One of them, through a medium, gives permission to begin the work. Then the evil spirits are brought, besetters of the persons who had appealed to the group, and possess the mediums but only one can talk each time. The director talks to every one of them, in order to know the reason why they pursue the sick. With arguments to make them understand that they are wrong, attempts are made, with the help of the good spirits, to obtain the voluntary removal of the spirits. Naturally, it is necessary that the director is well experienced in order to be able to influence the spirits. He must have moral and dialectical knowledge.

The healing work is complemented by means of passes administered by healing mediums (like Mr. Harry Edwards of Surrey).

What a lot of the sick have is an undisciplined psychic power which causes obsession. Most people do not accept the phenomena, many of them are Catholics or Protestants and they reject mediumship. The only way to free them from this difficult situation is that they decide to discipline that faculty which is inborn and which no-one can avoid.

In answer to questions which I sent him, S. Ferrari wrote again on the 3rd May 1961. Extracts from this letter are as follows:

1. Our Spiritual Hospital has actually a built area of 13,000 square metres. It is a building of reinforced concrete with several floors. It can take 176 patients now. It has some rooms and equipment for the necessary medical and psychic treatment including a surgery, to attend to request cases among interned mental patients. Our Hospital is dedicated only to the treatment of soul illnesses, i.e. mental and nervous.
2. The Hospital has on its service and paid, three doctors but, in 1960, 22 other psychiatrists attended their interned patients. We have contacts with Government Institutes to help their staff.
3. The Hospital is owned by an association formed by Spiritualists, organised in accordance with Brazilian laws. The members of the association contribute a certain sum each month. The Hospital also supports itself by collecting from the interned and treated patients in the proportion of 70% of the total capacity. The other 30% is used for free treatment of people with no financial means.
4. 90% of the treated patients are Catholics: some are Protestant or other religious persuasions. Real Spiritualists are very few, generally mediums who have been careless in controlling their mediumship and become victims of obsession.
5. Our Hospital treats exclusively mental and nervous illnesses, as I mentioned above, only treating other cases when they appear among the patients already having psychic treatment.
6. There are really many cases of pure schizophrenia and these can only be attended to by doctors, though we give them treatment by healing passes which help to strengthen the nervous centres. Cases of pure obsession are not unusual. Maybe 40% of the interned patients could be classified in this category. They are also attended by doctors because the obsession brings reflections on the somatic body. We give the same medical and psychic treatment in all cases trusted to the Hospital except those who are members of orthodox churches who ask for exclusive medical treatment.

7. I cannot inform you how many Spiritualist associations in my country are supported actively by doctors. My country has a very large territory and, personally, I do not maintain correspondence with the thousands of centres existent in several Brazilian states. I am sending you, enclosed, a list of 21 Spiritualist Hospitals of the same kind as ours, which treat obsession and also give medical assistance.
8. I believe they are all able to send you details of several cases of psychic healing. As I have already mentioned in my last letter, also in hundreds of Spiritualist Centres, cures of obsession are carried out with patients which do not have to be interned in hospitals. There is even a city with 10,000 inhabitants, more or less, all of them Spiritualists, which is visited by thousands of people from all parts of Brazil and even from other countries. The name of the city is Palmelo, near the new capital, Brazilia, and its mayor and spiritual leader is S. Jeronimo Candido Gomides.

Naturally, I was delighted to receive such valuable information which clearly revealed the enlightened approach by some members of the medical profession in Brazil.

The following extracts are taken from a long letter dated 10th June 1961 which I received from Iwao P. Hino of the Oomoto Foreign Mission Department, Kyoto-fu, Japan:

> We, followers of Oomoto, believe in possession by spirits both supreme and baser or ignorant . . .
>
> According to Oomoto's view everyone of us, who lives in such an age with the unnatural predominant position of flesh over spirit, has his spirit defiled or separated more or less. Thus possession by baser or ignorant spirits results . . .
>
> Those who believe in the existence of the spiritual world will recognize the possibility of possession by various spirits. A "medium" of the spiritual science is an example. In Shintoism, those who are possessed by spirits are called "Kan'unski" (owner of another spirit). But their possessed spirit may be quite various in kind; right or wrong, higher or lower. Therefore a discrimination is essential. Such mediator is called "Saniwa". It is needless to say that we cannot believe what the "Kan'unski" says without going through "Saniwa", namely severe discrimination.

A. M. Clauzure of Griandle, France replied to my enquiries in his letter dated 31st October 1961 and the relevant paragraphs of his letter are printed below:

> The study of obsession cases about which you wrote have a great importance. Spiritism with its knowledge and the possibility of speaking to the obsessing spirit through a medium makes it possible for the spirit to understand its failing and, therefore, to get to the core of the mental trouble. These cases are more frequent than one thinks. Here is what Allan Kardec said about this subject:
>
> "We must not confuse pathological madness with obsession: this one does not come from a cerebral lesion but from the subjugation bad spirits exercise on certain individuals which sometimes has the appearance of madness. This application, which is very frequent, does not derive from any spiritual belief and has existed from the beginning of time. In these cases, orthodox medicine is powerless and even hurtful. Spiritism, in making this new cause of mental trouble known, gives at the same time, the only way to overcome it by working, not on the patient, but on the obsessing spirit. Spiritism is the remedy, not the cause of the trouble."
>
> One of our friends, M. Emile Moreau, President of the Society of the Friends of the Spirit Association in Paris, has had the occasion several times with his experimental group to free obsession cases.

I wrote to M. Moreau and the following paragraphs are extracted from his letter dated 13th December 1961:

> Obsession is a very important fact that Spiritualists and Psychic Researchers cannot ignore nor pass under silence . . .
>
> I think it is necessary to remember certain practices relevant to the spirit people.
>
> 1. Death does not always transform human personality.
> 2. Besides certain very spiritually evolved beings, the majority of people leave the physical plane with the same mentality they had while living.
>
> In this last case a distinction must be made for persons having had during their lives a sincere spiritual element from the ones strictly materialistic.
>
> Death for the latter is not a break.

Their ideas, their thoughts carry on the same round in the etheric, exactly the same way as they did while on earth. This is the reason why it is very difficult to make these entities believe they are manifesting themselves through a trance medium and that they are dead to the physical plane.

For them, post mortem life is the same as the life they have in the sleep state, the ideas, the thoughts of the living subjects are the constitutional elements on which the mind of the deceased keeps on working.

If, in a general manner, we believe that the soul in leaving the body only takes the value of the good and bad actions, the elements which served in the formations of his character, in other words his mental body follows the soul after the separation with the physical body. That is the reason why, when these entities manifest themselves through a medium, their thoughts are in contact with the mechanism of a brain and they express themselves the same as when they were living without having a conscious feeling of the process.

In my group there was a Mr. B. who, in spite of living a righteous life seemed to have a lot of bad luck: business deals falling through at the last moment, unlucky happenings, depression with a fixed idea of suicide and diverse accidents.

One day, going on his bicycle, without any material reason, he fell off it receiving slight injuries. Several weeks after, when sitting in the group with a trance medium, a spirit manifested himself and addressed Mr. B. in violent terms, mentioned the bicycle accident and told him he was sorry he had not been able to cause him more harm at the time.

As leader of the group I let him talk his bitterness out and then tried to show him the stupidness of his arguments, calling to his better nature and showing that bad actions never pay. He became calmer and explained he wanted to revenge himself of the wrong that Mr. B. had done him in a previous life . . .

Helping the suffering spirits and trying to redeem those who are bad is a great moral task. To do this well, it is necessary that the one who takes up this work does it with a great love for those fallen beings. The love that one can give them and that they feel confusedly is the best remedy for their ignorance.

Other than in isolated cases, doctors do not accept this as a cure.

The countries in Latin America and especially Brazil and the Argentine where Spiritualism from the Kardec teachings is widely known, have for a long time tried to cure mental diseases through mediumship with a lot of success. Certain centres have hospitals where the doctors are Spiritualists and treat the mental patients in seances.

In a lot of cases, obsessions and mental diseases are found in individuals who have mediumistic tendencies.

M. Moreau enclosed the following report which was written by Dr. P. Jotopoulous, President of the Hellenique Society for the Study of Metaphysics and formerly a Professor at the University of Athens:

Towards the end of December 1910, living in Corfou, I learned that a young girl named Anne Vicatou, which I will in future indicate by the letter A. became mad after having the following dream: she was in a church where the priest had on his forehead two big horns and was reading a sacred book . . .

The fact that madness came after this sort of dream brought me to believe that this probably was an obsession case. I let the young girl's family know that I was prepared to give my help to try and cure her. After the family had accepted my offer, I went there. During the crisis, A's character was completely changing, from quiet and shy she was becoming rude, shouting inane things and her body had violent spasms. When the crisis was over A. could not remember anything. Her doctor prescribed sedatives which did not give any results. He then advised to put the patient in an asylum. During the crisis I was not addressing myself to A. but to the supposed obsessing spirit. I heard through the mouth of A. someone asking me, surprised, how was it I was attributing these speeches to someone else, this was followed with pertinent remarks.

For this reason I was repeating aloud that an obsessing spirit had taken control of A. and I was asking him in the name of God to leave. I was trying to tell him that, through persisting in staying, he would bring grave punishment on himself. Through my insistence, the obsessing spirit dropped his mask and said, "You are right, if you can, make me go"

Straight away I started praying for the patient and for the obsessing spirit as directed by Alan Kardec in his book *The Book of Mediums.*

After praying for a while I noticed that the crisis was subsiding. I left at the end of the day advising the family to avoid calling the doctor and to let me know immediately in the eventuality of a new crisis. The next day I saw the beginning of a new crisis and, as before, I prayed for A. and for the obsessing spirit. This resulted in stopping the crisis, leaving the patient weak and surprised at my presence. I told her I was her new doctor. During all January 1911 I went every day with the patient, praying each time, trying to tell the obsessing spirit that, through getting at A., he was really harming himself. After a time, the crises were not so strong and not so frequent.

An important fact is that, during the crises, A. was often using Italian with a Southern accent. Speaking Italian myself I used to answer the obsessing spirit in this language. One day, making a mistake, the spirit repeated the sentence accentuating the mistake. It must be noted that A. could hardly speak Italian. We found in the house an elementary Italian book where only the first six lessons seemed to have been studied.

The state of the patient was showing amelioration and the obsessing spirit was less hostile towards me. But he never gave his identity nor why he was obsessing A.

I had to leave Corfou to go to Athens. In consideration of the improvement of the patient I persuaded the family to take the patient to Athens so that I could carry on the treatment there. She went to an aunt of hers. This one was surprised that a lawyer was taking the place of a doctor and that this one was using strange methods to cure her niece.

Thinking I was an impostor, she asked a friend of hers who was a doctor to be present under some excuse. The doctor asked me what treatment I was using with the patient and I told him I thought I was in the presence of a split personality case, and in this case I was using the appropriate formula to get rid of the pathological personality which was produced by the patient and therefore, for myself, a foreign personality which is independent to the patient. I added that this divergence was only theoretically important if the formula employed, suggestion, prayer or order had the result of curing the patient. The doctor was of the same mind.

At this moment A., who had been very quiet, started to become nervous which was a sign that a crisis was on its way. The doctor asked me to leave the room during a few minutes. When I returned the patient was in a violent crisis. He asked me to bring her back to her normal state. I refused, asking him to do it himself. So with severity and with a loud voice he asked the patient to be quiet, which resulted in bringing the crisis to its paroxysm. The doctor asked me a second time to quieten the patient.

Addressing myself to the obsessing spirit in Italian, I asked him to make my work easier and to leave the patient. He said he was ready to stop annoying A. who could go back to Corfou shortly. The patient became quiet straight away, surprising the doctor and her uncle. The next day the doctor asked A's aunt to call on him and told her that A., in his opinion, was simulating the illness and that I was an accomplice in this farce because in his opinion it was not possible to calm a patient with the method I was using.

A. and her aunt returned to Corfou, the crises become less frequent and when I saw her again at Easter she was completely cured.

I end this report with the following observations: A lot of people shut up in mental hospitals as suffering from mental diseases are only obsessed. To be interned is not helping them but often makes matters worse through their contact with other obsessing spirits. The cures which can happen are not always due to medical treatments.

(P. Yotopoulous).

In January 1964, I received an enquiry from Dr. Ian Stevenson, M.D., Professor of Psychiatry at the University of Virginia. He requested any information I could give him concerning the use of mediums in treating mentally ill persons. In his letter he wrote:

Two years ago I was in Brazil. While there I spent a day

> with Dr. Ignacio Ferreira, the director of a Spiritualist Psychiatric Hospital in Uberaba, Minas Geraes. I observed the medium he works with in one of her trances and went round seeing the patients with Dr. Ferreira who uses no drugs or electric shock treatment whatever and approaches all cases from the spiritistic point of view. Obviously from what I saw I had no basis for evaluating what he was doing. But I do believe in survival of physical death, which means believing in discarnate spirits. And I think it quite possible that *some* mental illness, perhaps a great deal, is related to noxious influences from discarnate spirits. At any rate this is something I very much want to look into further with an open mind, because I think it may have very great promise for future treatment.

It was encouraging to have a direct link from a doctor who had made a short acquaintance with the work of Dr. Ferreira at Uberaba.

In a further letter, Dr. Stevenson wrote:

> The reason you did not hear from Dr. Ignacio Ferreira is not that he is too busy, although he is, but that he speaks and writes no English. I have only a couple of letters from him myself and both in Portuguese.

In a further letter in February 1965, he wrote:

> I continue extremely interested in the study of cases which may be due to possessions, and I plan as soon as possible and when opportunities present to make a more intensive study of the question here.

It seemed incredible that a layman, like myself, could obtain information about the treatment of mental cases in other countries by doctors who are aware of the possibility of interference by ignorant spirits and yet there appears to be little or no recognition of this possibility in Great Britain. I feel that a Commission of Enquiry should be sent from Great Britain to Brazil to obtain facts concerning the results of treatment with the use of mediums in the Spiritualist hospitals. If good results are being obtained, then, surely, such treatment should be available to sufferers in Great Britain?

It seems very clear that there is a vacuum in our orthodox treatment of mental illness. Does this vacuum exist because many psychiatrists are atheists and are, therefore, unable to guide sufferers back to a state of wholeness with complete harmony between body, mind and spirit?

By 1965, greater interest was being taken in these deeper aspects of mental illness and the Churches' Fellowship for Psychical and Spiritual Studies had formed two Sub-Committees on Mental Illness. The special information which I had obtained was passed to the leaders of these Sub-Committees and regarded as valuable. A direct link was made with Dr. Ignacio Ferreira of Umberaba and he gave permission for the translation of his books, *Reincarnation Face to Face with Psychiatry* and *A New Approach to Medicine,* and for publication in Great Britain. Unfortunately, the records of his cases of mental illness due to spirit possession were not written in a manner which would convince members of the B.M.A. in Great Britain.

Mrs. Anne Dooley, a journalist who visited Brazil on a psychic quest in 1967 paid tribute to the spiritual progress she found there in a lecture which she gave at the C.F.P.S.S. conference in September 1968.

She said that Dr. Ferreira of Uberaba and Dr. Ferrari of Porto Alegre both believe it would be of great value if a commission of British medical men and open-minded psychic researchers could be persuaded to go out to Brazil and study the work now being carried out in the Spiritist hospitals, frequently under appalling difficulties. She thought that, in Brazil, we may well be witnessing the birth of a true civilisation which has turned its back on both nuclear war and racial colour bars. A civilisation which will be based upon a flowering of man's psychic and spiritual faculties, dedicated to peace and service to one's fellowmen.

PART II

Some Trends in the Seventies

I

RENEWED VITALITY AND THE CHURCH

Another important event in my life occured in 1964 when I retired from the Civil Service. As I held a secure position in the executive grade with a good salary, good holidays and good working conditions and would not reach the retirement age of 65 until 1973, this would appear to many people to be an irrational step to take. I had no firm reason for making this change but was acting on a subtle feeling which suggested that, if I could retire with a small pension, I would only need to work part-time in order to live moderately and meet my material needs. This would give me more time for my personal interests and activities. On looking back, I now regard this step as one of the most important events in my life as, once again, the change opened up avenues of experience which proved to be of inestimable value.

Readers of Part I may have assumed that, as a result of my personal experiences in the psychic field, I became and remained a keen supporter of the Spiritualist movement. This was not so. After my retirement, I drew more closely to the work of the Churches' Fellowship for Psychical and Spiritual Studies, becoming Regional Organiser for the Southern counties covering the area from Oxfordshire to Hampshire and from West Sussex to Dorset. In 1968, as a result of my efforts in the southern region, I became General Secretary of the Fellowship. During this period I was studying Christianity as an adult and comparing the writings of Christian scholars with the philosophy given by authors in the Spiritualist movement. *Gradually, I realised that, when I was previously a strong supporter of Spiritualism as a religion and a keen critic of the Church, I was ignorant of the depths and richness of Christianity and was depending on the limited understanding of it which I had gained as a child.* I realised that this applied to most people as very few take the trouble to study Christianity as an adult.

At the same time, I was conscious of the power of the knowledge gained through psychic research in giving people a deeper understanding of life and, therefore, a purpose in life. My work for the Fellowship with its splendid motto "To Faith Add Knowledge" taught me how this special knowledge could give a deeper meaning to Christian teachings and to many phrases used in the services of worship. I found that many other people were following the same course as myself by investigating psychic research and returning to the Church with a new understanding.

It became clear to me that the Church embodies the central knowledge of life after death, guidance from the next world and the expression of the Holy Spirit through spiritual gifts but it has failed to communicate this knowledge to the man-in-the-street. In these circumstances, it is not surprising that there has been a loss of faith and a decline in church attendance.

Some examples of phrases in common use which are given a deeper meaning by the knowledge gained through psychic research are:

"as it is in heaven."
"Angels, archangels and the whole company of heaven."
"The Communion of Saints."
"The power of the Holy Spirit."
"Angel Hosts guiding us here below."

If we examine the words of the hymns appropriate to the Anglican festival of St. Michael and all Angels, we find constant references to angels hosts guiding us in our daily lives. So here is a situation where churchgoers sing about this guidance as a reality but they are not encouraged to discuss the subject. As guidance on all spiritual matters is given by the clergy, I suggest that this situation reveals some serious omissions in the training at our theological colleges.

After attending a special conference on psychical studies and healing for the clergy, a young curate wrote to me saying that the conference was like water to a man dying of thirst in the desert!

The reader will, by now, appreciate that I have a special

interest in the emergence and development of patterns of thought which aid the spiritual progress of mankind. It seems evident to me that the formation and steady growth of the Fellowship comes under this heading. Having participated in meetings and conferences in all parts of the country and met and corresponded with many individuals including those in other countries, I have no doubt that the work of the Fellowship is meeting a special need. As the development of Spiritualism as a religion blocked the spreading of the knowledge to the Church, it was inevitable that another pattern of growth such as the Fellowship should emerge. It has the support of many bishops as well as leaders of the Free Churches and its members are advised to study psychical research in the light of Christian teachings. Branches are formed which hold monthly meetings and they organise many groups for study, discussion, healing, meditation, etc.

The loss of vitality in the Church can be related, I suggest, to the loss of a real understanding of the phrase "The power of the Holy Spirit." There are many examples of the power operating in the lives of the Apostles and early Christians, but few examples of it operating among church members today. An experience which I had in London confirmed that this view was also held within the Church. One day, feeling the need to enter a church during my lunch hour, I entered Westminster Cathedral which was near my office. Before leaving I browsed over the bookstall and bought a copy of the current issue of a magazine called *Sunday*. When I read it, I was surprised to find that it contained a satirical article on Pentecost in an English village bearing the caption "Death of the Holy Ghost" together with the words from the well-known hymn "Come, Holy Ghost our souls inspire and lighten with celestial fire." The following extract reveals the writer's approach on the subject:

> If, however, our hearts had leaped up during the Gospel, they soon crawled down again in the sermon. Ingeniously avoiding anything directly controversial the preacher sought, by understatement and innuendo, to make certain that whatever strange, scandalous things the Holy Spirit may have done on a previous occasion, He certainly would not be allowed to go on like that here! The still, small voice, the hidden

operation, yes — but nothing demonstrative, emotional, bizarre . . .

Well, thought I, one does not have to be a "Pentecostalist" to realise that, so far as the average parson and his flock are concerned, Pentecost might not have happened. As the calm, monotonous voice went on piling platitude upon platitude with deadly skill, one could sense the conventional fear that, having been evoked, the Holy Ghost might even now take us at our word, the divine ruach rushing mightily like a hot wind through the deserts of our souls. Fear, too, that on the heads of parson and choir, sidesmen, stiff colonels and respectable elderly ladies, there would indeed rest cloven tongues like as of fire. Even more disconcerting, we might find ourselves jabbering away uncontrollably in all kinds of foreign lingoes. How un-English — how very embarrassing! . . .

On went the sermon, systematically ironing out every possibility of there ever being a latter day Pentecost in our Church. Spirit of the living God! I exclaimed within myself, is *this* all that Pentecost means? We who claim to be truly descended from the Apostles of old — why are we not also clothed with power from on high? Where in this day and age are the "signs following" — the mighty works, the casting out of demons, the healing of the sick and raising of the dead? Before me there unfolded the vision of a Church triumphant, filled with the Holy Spirit, reaching out into the world and making men whole and strong and saved in the name of the Risen Lord Jesus; a church of glad and generous hearts praising and blessing God as they broke the bread and prayed together . . .

As I left the church, a group in the porch was discussing volubly with considerable more feeling than knowledge, the relative merits of "old" and "new" services. It was plain they had already forgotten about Pentecost. Outside, I looked for the crowd, cut to the heart by the burning words of the Gospel and the cataclysm of wind and fire, asking urgently of themselves "Brethren, what shall we do?"

But the village street was completely empty and there was not even the sound of a "still, small voice!"

In view of this unexpected experience, it was not surprising that, within a week, when browsing around the S.P.C.K. bookshop in London, I bought a copy of the book *The Spirit Within You* by A. M. Stibbs and J. I. Packer. The note on the outer back cover read "The Holy Spirit has been called 'the neglected member of the Trinity'. In this book the authors plead for a return to a fully biblical and dynamic concept of his works. If their contention is true that God's 'free Spirit' has been shackled in Anglican forms of rites, then this trenchant little book may make a major contribution to the modern renewal of the Church!"

These experiences excited my interest in the Holy Spirit as it seemed to me that the main job of the Fellowship was to restore this power to the Church.

The first Maurice Elliott Memorial Lecture was delivered to members of the Fellowship by the Rev. Professor J. Macdonald, M.A., B.D., S.T.M., Ph.D., of Glasgow University. In this lecture he stated:

> St. Paul groups a number of supernormal experiences together and calls them gifts of the Holy Spirit. He belonged, we are led to believe to a new era, a new dispensation. So do we, we are likewise told. How can it be that the presence of the Holy Spirit is not now normally accompanied by the gifts of the Holy Spirit? Indeed, if a churchman today were to say that while under the influence of the Holy Spirit he saw visions or heard voices, he would at once be relegated to the status of the mentally unbalanced.
>
> Is there not something unwholesome and illogical about this state of affairs? How does it happen in the age of the new dispensation begun by Christ that the Holy Spirit is here and yet the fruits of the Holy Spirit, as understood by St. Paul, are not here? Where are the fruits of the Holy Spirit and where can the enquiring young christians of our generation find the gifts of the Holy Spirit? Is it not true that the Church of today is largely at the New Testament stage, having failed to progress beyond it?"

In the ninth Maurice Elliott Lecture, the Rev. Dr. K. G. Cuming, M.R.C.S., L.R.C.P., now Chairman of the C.F.P.S.S. said that he regarded the Fellowship as a kind of catalyst for the Spirit, whose function it was to reactivate the Church with spiritual power. He was quite convinced that the Fellowship had been called into being by the Spirit for good reasons, as part of an integral plan on a vast canvas for the spiritual upliftment and re-education of the world. He urged members to return to their churches as the Fellowship could be an agent of the Light, sending the rays of spiritual and intellectual enlightenment, as a lighthouse does, out into the darkness of mind and spirit. He advocated the provision of a kind of school of the prophets.

Dr. Cuming's reference to the spiritual role of the Fellowship in the world makes one wonder why this development should take place in Britain?

During my period of work as General Secretary, our President was Chancellor the Rev. E. Garth Moore, M.A., J.P., who was Director of Studies in Law at Corpus Christi College, Cambridge. In an address on "The Christian Faith and Psychical Research" given at the Annual Conference of the Southern Region at Torquay in October 1970 he said:

> In so far as the attitudes of the more orthodox Christian bodies has been hostile, it has of recent years been hostile, I think, because of a confusion between psychical research and Spiritualism, which of course are really two distinctly different things . . .
>
> Attitudes have changed from different times. In the middle Ages, by which in this context I mean roughly the year 900 AD to, let us say, 1450 AD it isn't perhaps generally realised that whatever may have been the strictly official attitude of the Catholic Church (it was in fact in process of being formed), there was a very considerable body of thought of a considerable body of persons who would have by no means been hostile . . .
>
> From our point of view and the one with any relevance to what we are discussing this morning, is the fact, the undoubted fact, that the attitude of the Church, for practical purposes at any rate, whatever may have been the original tenets, was at that particular time, one of at least toleration.

Referring to the prohibitions against witchcraft, etc., in Exodus and Deuteronomy, he pointed out that there is a complete superceding of the prohibitions in the Acts of the Apostles, and you can't just pick and choose extracts from the Bible, anything there is of immense value, but it is to be interpreted with due regard to the way and time in which it was written as we have fresh insights into what is right conduct which are largely due to what we read in the New Testament. He also said:

> And then you have our Lord's own — I was going to say astonishing — psychic gifts. I do not like using that expression — call it what you will. You see our Lord exhibiting what in others we should call psychic gifts, the gift of healing for example; but (possibly more to the point of our present discussion) extra-sensory perception. "He needed no man to tell Him what was in man." You see that more strikingly, perhaps in the story of the woman of Samaria . . . One sees I think from it all the very important fact that although our Lord was exceptional in the extent of the manifestations which He displayed, He was true man. He was perfect man. He was showing us what man was created to be — a reflection of the Divine . . . He was showing us what man can still be, if he will properly align himself with God . . . Man's attributes include the ability to demonstrate what we call today psychic phenomena, as an absolute matter of course. That these are natural attributes is pretty obvious, from our Lord's own reaction. Occasionally He would rely upon the mighty works which He performed as being things which would interest people, but they were rare occasions. On the whole He did not wish to win men that way, or to be regarded as a wonder-worker. He did His works of healing, not because He went out into the world to heal, but as they came His way in what you may call ordinary neighbourly activity — a person came His way and was in need of help and He said "The works that I do, greater works than these shall ye do." And so, I think, He was showing us what is in man and what we should cultivate. And when you come to the Acts of the Apostles you will find in the miracles performed by the Apostles recorded in that book, the immediate fulfilment of what our Lord said — that other people should do this sort of thing. But you don't find it today? My guess is that it is because

very few of us today are anything like so committed to God as were the very early disciples, certainly the Apostles . . .

The subtle danger of Spiritualism is the temptation to substitute something far, far lower for a search for God. The temptation to take the alleged communications through the medium from those who are dead as though they were necessarily gospel, or indeed true. As you well know they are very often pretty ropey, and there is a very real danger that they should be accorded a degree of credibility which they do not deserve.

I don't think myself that provided all the obvious precautions are taken and provided you are as near being a well-balanced person as anybody can be — if anyone really is — I don't think that there can be any condemnation of psychical research. "The Heavens declare the glory of God and the firmament telleth His handiworks" said the Psalmist. "By their fruits shall they be known", said our Lord. They are saying the same thing. The fruits of God are His creation. We learn of God by observing His creation, and if only humanity hadn't fallen we should learn best of God by observing man. As it is, we learn best of God by observing His Incarnate Son.

The Fellowship consists of members of all denominations, the majority being recorded as Anglican, although this does not necessarily mean that they are active church-goers. It may be that many are treading a similar pathway to myself. They are all seekers after truth, the knowledge gained when they open their minds to the value of psychical research can lead them back to the Church where they can add to the renewal of vitality which is already taking place.

The following extracts from letters which I received from members and enquirers express what many people feel:

From Surrey: "for many years I have been a keen student of psychic and allied subjects and regard the Fellowship as the most important movement in the history of the Church. Regretably, the question of survival, surely the most fundamental doctrine of any religion, has tended to be regarded as "unknowable" and, as such, has been given little attention as compared with other doctrines. This has resulted, within my own experience, in many practising Christians, laity and clergy, having little more than a vague hope of a future life and in some cases being actually hostile to any investigation. Thus, the Fellowship has a most important mission . . . I utilize every suitable opportunity to make known the existence of the movement."

From Sussex: "I think that the churches can do marvels and with the 'new' approach to psychic matters I do believe that the numbers in the congregations will swell, because if folk can be made to see that thoughts and actions every minute of each day really do matter from a personal evolutionary point of view to say the least, then I can see religion really meaning something to people. It is so important to make people realise that religion is an affair of every minute and not just a Sunday business; and what we think and do so important whereas the lip service, confessions, etc., are so meaningless in themselves."

From Canada: "I was very interested to see your advertisement and want to let you know how delighted I am to discover there is such an organisation as your Fellowship. I have been interested in Psychical Research for years, and feel very strongly that the Church should pay more attention to this field of study and its relevance to our faith. *It's like a breath of fresh air to realise there are others like myself who wish to pursue Psychical Research in a Christian setting.*"

From Wiltshire: "I have been interested in these subjects for many years, I have studied many mediums and read dozens and dozens of books. I have attended untold seances and privately experienced strange things which suggest survival. I also do a lot of inspirational writing. I have done healing — one chap whose hands were crippled with arthritis was nearly normal a year later. I have been told by dozens of mediums that I possess healing powers. However, this healing does seem to work. In spite of this, I was brought up in the Church of England and *I don't want to belong to any cult. My ambition is to see the Mother Church living in the twentieth century. I am sure that Jesus Christ would want this were he walking the earth today.*"

From Hampshire: "I have recently become very interested in life after death and the possible effect knowledge of this 'life' could have on our lives in this world. I feel in the light of knowledge of this kind everyday religion could be given the added spark it so urgently needs in order to attract more people's attention and attendance in Church."

From Jersey: "I am convinced that the Holy Spirit is moving amongst the many people who find themselves in great difficulties with regard to the established Church. I am sure that your work is blessed and meant to prosper, and I feel proud that I have been guided to join the Fellowship. When I saw you, I had the distinct impression that this must have been how the Church started and now, at the end, comes a new beginning. I cannot get rid of a feeling of anticipation as if I must be ready, quite what for I don't know, but of one thing I am certain, whatever it will be it will be quite world shattering, perhaps it is just foolishness but I wondered if we were going to experience a new revelation."

From Oxfordshire: "My husband and I have been actively interested in these matters for upwards of thirty years. To us, they are the things that really matter in this more and more difficult and material world of today. Both of us were brought up in the Christian orthodox teaching and are by no means divorced from it. Indeed I feel that such teaching led me to these deeper things . . . I have had many personal experiences. The Great Book is chock full of all such and what people are pleased to call 'miracles' still happen today and as to mediumship — the words of St. Paul still hold! And why not? *Oh, it is so important for the Church to 'look again' and interpret these matters with less dogma and creed — therefore, I am overjoyed at this Fellowship and only wish I could do more to help. Our beautiful churches — steeped in the worship of centuries — are the rightful places for the Divine Revelation and all Healing.*"

From Oxfordshire: "Your remark about this new vitality being based in the Church in Great Britain touches me personally. As a former fugitive from Nazi-German persecution I have always felt deeply thankful for the spiritual sanctuary of these isles."

From a teacher in Northumberland following an unsought psychic experience when holidaying in Scotland: "Certainly with me, the disturbing fact was that I was having to reorganise and discard many of the ideas I had had about the non-existence of spirits and I did not find it easy. It has raised so many questions in my mind. Where, previously, I had found it extremely difficult to believe that there was anything after death, I must now accept that there was (if I am to believe my own eyes). *Because I must now accept the spiritual world exists, it has, for the first time become easy to believe that God exists also.*"

From a schoolboy in London aged 12½: "I would be very grateful if you could send me some information on psychical phenomena because I am going to do a talk on it for my form."

The steady flow of letters like these gave me a great sense of privilege in working at the centre of these signs of a spiritual awakening which was centred in Britain and I have come to believe that, as this growing awareness spread in the Church in Britain, so it would automatically spread to all parts of the world where we had formed Christian links in the past.

I have no doubt that this awareness opens channels in people which will allow the power of the Holy Spirit to enter and be expressed in their daily lives according to their individual abilities. At the end of the Anglican service of Holy Communion those taking part say the following prayer:

> Almight God, we offer Thee our souls and bodies, to be a living sacrifice through Jesus Christ our Lord. *Send us out into the world in the power of Thy Spirit to live and work to Thy praise and glory.*

If this prayer is repeated without understanding, it may be meaningless and ineffectual. If, on the other hand, it is said as a renewed covenant with God and a knowledge of some of the ways in which the power for good operates through the guidance of "Angel Hosts" and the "company of Heaven", it can release a power which becomes a reality. To use a simple analogy, if an offer of service to God is made sincerely from the heart, it goes up to spiritual planes like a light. Those who are part of the "Heavenly Civil Service" receive the offer and carry it into practical reality by telepathic impressions so that the person making the offer is guided to meet those whom he or she can help or from whom help can be received for the promotion of the Divine Plan.

When working as a Regional Organiser for the Fellowship, I made arrangements to visit Dorset in connection with the formation of a new branch. On my way from Berkshire, I had a lunch-time appointment with a member at Eastleigh during which I hoped to discuss the situation concerning the branch at Southampton. However, I believe that my intentions were over-ruled from the Other Side. During the morning of my visit, the lady at Eastleigh heard a voice which told her to contact a local clergyman and to ask him if he would like to meet me. She acted on the instruction and he agreed. He was the editor of the local edition of *Bridge*, a monthly newspaper incorporating national Christian news. As a result of this interference in my affairs, instead of discussing the local situation, I found myself telling the clergyman about the work of the Fellowship in general. The outcome was that he published an article on the Fellowship with the caption "Life after Death" in the November, 1967 issue. As the article would be read by many local people of all denominations, it is clear that those on the Other Side who arranged our meeting knew best. This example reminds us, of course, that Samuel, too, heard a voice and confirms the Christian teaching of guidance by angel hosts in our daily lives. Furthermore, the example emphasises the importance in our lives of those experiences which happen to us, often unexpectedly, and often beyond our control. It seems to me that an awareness of the possibility of such guidance introduces a greater degree of response in us and also a greater degree of adaptability. It is generally accepted that the power of God operates through people and it seems perfectly logical to extend this thought to include those who are still vital and alive although they have no physical body.

In November, 1967 I received a letter from one of our members in Berkshire whom I knew to be a well-balanced, intelligent person. In her letter she wrote, "Recently, I had occasion to write to the vicar of Dorchester Abbey and told him of a vision I had there in a Eucharist Service when I saw kneeling beside the vicar, a bishop with rows of monks behind him. Truly, we are surrounded by a 'cloud of witnesses'." The existence of the faculty of clairvoyance in some people but latent and potential in many people is a fact. In view of the patterns of events with which I have been associated, I believe that the existence of the Fellowship will result in more church members having clairvoyant or other similar experiences during services of worship. The study of psychical research raises an awareness in the mind which can be a prelude to supernormal experience.

In March, 1969 the minister of a Congregational Church in Western Australia wrote, "I was astonished to read that the churches in England were so far ahead in these matters and I thank God for it. We in our church have an active group drawn from many denominations doing exactly what you are describing in your magazine. We have our Conferences, our Study Groups, our Healing Services and many, many people are interested in this and come to these meetings and services. We have attracted a great many young people who come from many walks of life, including many university students".

One of the interesting aspects of my job at the Head Office of the Fellowship was the contact with members overseas. This contact was maintained usually by correspondence but we also had visitors from overseas from time to time. At the time of the Lambeth Conference of bishops from all parts of the world in 1968, we sent a letter to each of them.

There was an immediate response from the Assistant Bishop of Ibadan, Nigeria who visited the Head Office and joined the Fellowship. As a result he wrote an article on the work of the Fellowship which was published in the June, 1969 issue of *The Nigerian Christian*. In it he wrote:

> I commend membership of this Fellowship to the clergy and lay members of the Church. It will help to deepen our spiritual and devotional life. I am convinced that in these days of materialism when many people, not excepting professing Christians of our Church, show little or no interest in things spiritual, the Fellowship has much to teach us, not least in the realm of spiritual healing . . .
>
> "Serious research", writes the Organising Secretary of the Fellowship, "reveals that psychic phenomena are not evil as many church members believe. It is another power which is part of the great phenomena of Nature and, like atomic power, electricity, etc., it can be used for the benefit of mankind when it is understood and controlled by responsible people".

Also in 1969, I received letters from a young American in Austria. She wrote:

I am an opera singer beginning my career in Vienna. I came to Vienna last year and wasn't interested at all in the Church. Before the college years I was active in the American Episcopal Church but gradually disintegrated spiritually until last fall when I found God again through the Anglican Church in Vienna. Shortly after my conversion I began noticing that, when I prayed, my hands would get very warm. This was very unusual since my hands were normally cold, especially in cold weather. Now, I walk into an ice-cold church, hands freezing, and in a few minutes of prayer they are pulsing with heat. It becomes stronger during intercessory prayer when I picture someone being healed of some physical or spiritual ills.

She described two cases of people in pain which went away after she put her hands on the affected areas. She then wrote:

I don't know if this can be explained in some other way, but if I am to have some power in my hands, I wish to use it to help people and to glorify God. But I don't know what to do about it, or if I should do anything at all. If you could offer a few suggestions, I would appreciate it greatly.

This example again shows clearly how the power of the Holy Spirit is breaking through ordinary men and women, and the great need for guidance which is not always available within the Church.

Many people criticise ritual in church services as it appears to be meaningless to them. In *Simple Guide to Psychic Laws*, Olivia Wigram writes:

To some people ritualism appears but a ridiculous mummery, and therefore to expect them to derive any benefit from attending a High Mass is absurd. To others the bareness of a dissenting Chapel renders religious exaltation impossible: equally for them chapel-going would be useless as a means of spiritual edification.

It may be asked, why have churches and chapels at all? Why not worship the Almighty under the blue of His sky, amid the incomparable glory of His works beside which the finest cathedral is but a shoddy effort?

The answer is that a focussing point is required, and that a building makes an easier one than an open space. To concentrate any force it must be confined, limited; a religious service is but the means of bringing the Divine Forces into concentrated effect, and every sect has, in its Communion Service, the culminating moment of that concentration which signifies the downpouring of the energies of the highest plane.

The achievement of this is simply and solely a magical one, for there is "White" magic as well as "Black". Certain movements and sounds create certain vibrations which affect the Auras of the worshippers, bringing their bodies, Etheric, Astral and Thought into line, and so stilling their restless movements. The officiating priest acts as their representative in whom are gathered up their combined intention, and the bread and wine he consecrates become the focussing point for the Divine Rays, just as a piece of glass will bring to a head the heat disseminated all round the sun . . .

Those who are clairvoyantly gifted may watch for themselves all that takes place during the celebration of Mass; not only the stilling and brightening of the auras of those assembled, but at the moment of concentration the streaming down of the dazzling light which is produced by the inconceivable rapid vibrations of the God-sent force, which so changes the etheric body of the wafer, that its particles do indeed undergo re-arrangement and become the vessels of the Logos, the Essence of Life, and as such radiate out over all that is near.

A further example of the way in which this knowledge is spreading was the publishing of an article on the Fellowship in *Church News* (an inset to parish magazines) in September 1969. It contained the following paragraphs:

To the outsider, the logic for the reason for the Fellowship is often overlooked! Yet who more than the Church of Christ should, in fact, be examining these questions? And if there is danger in such matters, then who more than the Church should be the vanguard? Who else should investigate? Who other should be on the spot to ensure against false and spurious teaching? In fact, where else should she be than just there where she thinks evil threatens the flock of Christ? We are bidden to grow in grace, not remain babes in Christ (Heb. 6: 1-3). The Fellowship exists to endeavour adequately to meet the intellectual and spiritual needs of her children today, and that there might be a wider understanding of the need to "go on to perfection". The motto of the Fellowship is "To Faith add Knowledge" and prayer, study and meditation groups all over the country seek to do just this scriptural bidding.

I have already referred to the letter which was sent to every bishop attending the Lambeth Conference in 1968. It was written by the Vice-Chairman of the Fellowship, the Rev. Canon J. D. Pearce-Higgins, M.A., Vice-Provost of Southwark and, for some years, Chairman of the Modern Churchmen's Union. In it, he wrote:

We feel that the Church is failing today not so much because of lack of devotion or of Samaritan service to the community, which it partly exists to provide or stimulate, but also on account of its failure to attract people by not giving them adequately apologetic answers to the problem of Life and Death which it also exists to provide. *In the light of what is known about the material universe as well as of the functioning of the human "psyche", especially as interpreted by Jung, we feel that the answers to the great problems of life and death, as taught in the theological colleges today, and as proclaimed from the pulpits, are inadequate to meet the needs of intelligent modern men and women . . .*

We believe that the age of miracles (however interpreted) is not dead. We believe that the arm of the Lord is not shortened even for man "come of age", and that where dedicated souls or charismatic gifts are found, there He can find channels for healing as well as for preaching and teaching according to the best traditions of the Church. We feel that the Lord's threefold command to preach, to teach and to heal has too often been whittled down to two, and that a Healing Church would carry more weight in the world . . .

We would further urge that the study of Parapsychology as being a department of Natural Theology, should be taken into the orbit of the theological faculties of universities and colleges, and we believe that by so doing we should increase the love, devotion and serviceableness of the Church to the needs of our time and generation, and do much to help to recover the "lost radiance of Christianity" which was surely based on the belief that "underneath are the everlasting arms" and that death is not the end of consciousness . . .

A return to a positive and rational belief in continued survival after death, in the form in which St. Paul held it, in a spiritual body, with all that this entails in the way of personal accountability as well as the hope of the bliss of Eternal Life, might well rejuvenate the Church, help to heal its divisions, enlighten its often obscure and irrelevant liturgies, and help to let its light so shine that the nations of the world, who after two thousand years of Christianity still sit in darkness and in the shadow of death, might be led to find joy and peace.

Canon Pearce-Higgins has been an outspoken champion for the work of the Fellowship and it was, therefore, not surprising that, in 1970, he was invited by the Liturgical Commission of the Anglican Church to submit suggested revised forms of service and prayers for funerals.

In an article, "Why think about Heaven?" which was published in the *Methodist Recorder* in November 1969, H. Cecil Pawson quoted the following passage from the anthology of C. S. Lewis:

> If you read history, you will find that the Christians who did most for the present world were just those who thought most of the next . . . It is since Christians have largely ceased to think of the other world they have become so ineffective in this.

Mr. Pawson wrote, " No one need care less — on the contrary I believe he will care more — for the needy in our world here, if he gives thought from time to time to the eternal city of God. The finest blueprint for life on earth is the vision of heaven.'Thy will be done on earth *as it is done in heaven*'."

Dr. D. M. A. Leggett, M.A., D.Sc., F.R.Ae.S., F.I.M.A., Vice-Chancellor of Surrey University, gave strong support to the Fellowship. During an address to a congregation of 800 at Guildford Cathedral in October 1967, he related how he and his mother had freely discussed death and possible after-life conditions shortly before her passing in December, 1959. As a result of this discussion, they agreed that if she found it possible to give him some indication of her continued existence, she would do so. In July 1961, he attended a conference on "Intimations of Reality" where he met a woman who was gifted with psychic powers but she was not a professional medium. One day, when they were chatting after lunch, she told him that his mother was present and gave him an intimate message which he accepted as confirmation of his mother's continued existence. His address was reported in the *Surrey Advertiser and County Times* and also in *Psychic News*.

Having an interest in new patterns of thought which emerge naturally to stimulate the spiritual progress of mankind, I have observed that it is often the case that one person appears to be the chosen instrument to be used to "trigger off" a new pattern. In the case of the Fellowship, the chosen instrument was Lt. Col. R. M. Lester, F.J.I. who became its Founder-Chairman for the first 18 years of its existence. After the death of his first wife, he met Air Marshal Lord Dowding who recommended him to carry out a personal investigation into survival after death. As he was a journalist, Col. Lester kept short-hand notes of his experiences and these enabled him to write a book called *In Search of the Hereafter*. As soon as the book was published, he began to receive a steady flow of letters from people who had read the book and who wanted to know more about the subject. Many of the letters came from church members and clergymen and this clearly revealed that the Church was not meeting their needs. It was from a nucleus of these people that the Fellowship was formed. In January, 1970, he reported that, after taking part in the Battle of the Somme in World War I, he saw no purpose in anything and was an agnostic. It was psychical research which brought him back to the Church. He said that the Fellowship had 77 branches in Great Britain and members in 25 other countries. In 1969, he and Mrs. Lester travelled 10,000 miles on Fellowship lectures and journeys and his post averaged 100 letters a week. They had carried out overseas tours in Scandinavia, U.S.A. and South Africa.

In July and August, 1966, the *National Christian Weekly News* published articles on the work of the Fellowship. The General Secretary at that time was the Rev. Bertram Woods, a Methodist minister. During an interview, he stated:

Many people who accept the study of psychic happenings are saddened by the vague and inadequate teachings of the Christian Churches about death. I have known eminent clergymen completely broken down because of the death of someone they love. That's because when it comes to the point much orthodox teaching is empty and carries no ring of truth.

There is a widespread feeling that death is an area which ought to be left in the unknown and not tampered with. We believe that, where the faith of the Christian can be confirmed and substantiated by facts, we ought to seek the facts and appeal to them.

In dealing with Dr. Robert Crookall's collection of accounts of life after death, the newspaper reported:

When the spirit body has been met into the spirit world, there is normally a period of rest which occupies a length of time which we would regard as perhaps three days. It takes time for a person to get used to a spirit body, and to recuperate from debilitating illness.

After this comes a form of judgment which is envisaged in every religion. One communicator said that the judgment consists in being able to see ourselves as we are, and by no stretch of imagination being able to avoid seeing it. It is a judgment of God upon us (lesser selves) through our higher selves . . . For many it is a terrible hour . . . directly one has realised how, where and why one was wrong, there is an instinctive feeling that one must work it out. And this way of recovery is in helping others who have exactly similar limitations, difficulties or vices.

In his Introduction to his book *Religious Faith and Twentieth-Century Man,** F. C. Happold writes:

Something is happening in the world. We are conscious of it all around us. Our era is said to be the era of the emergence of "secular man", man who has "come of age" and has no longer any need of "God". This may be true; but may it not also be the era of the emergence of a new sort of spiritual man?

Following a comment on the challenges to religious faith raised by the Bishop of Woolwich and Sir Julian Huxley, Happold writes:

* Penguin Books Ltd.

Even when allowances are made for that element of sensationalism which is characteristic of a great deal of the Press, *it was clear that, in spite of a growing secularism, a deep and widespread interest in religion still exists, but that the ways in which religious faith and belief are often expressed have little meaning or effect* . . . If one considers the present situation from the point of view of Christianity, it seems to be as follows: "Christianity now faces a crisis not dissimilar to that which it was called upon to face in its beginnings".

Many people have compared these signs of spiritual awakening with the activities during the days of the early Church. The examples I have given reveal that the power of the Holy Spirit is no respecter of persons and that it is flowing to a greater degree through ordinary men and women. At the same time, changes are taking place within the Church which allow the laity greater opportunities. In my opinion, it is essential that the laity become better informed about the reality of spiritual gifts today as in the early days of the Church. If this knowledge is not given from the pulpit (the proper place for spiritual instruction), it will continue to flow through bodies like the Fellowship.

As an Anglican with an enquiring mind, I have often wondered why so many Epistles containing wonderful stories from the Acts of the Apostles have been allocated in the Prayer Book to weekday services. As a result, they are rarely the subjects for sermons.

II

EDUCATION, MEDICINE AND SCIENCE

It must be obvious to everyone that the way in which we act depends largely on what we know and what we believe. In Part I, and also in the preceding chapter, I have tried to show the value of the knowledge gained through psychical research in extending our knowledge about Life. This results in the raising of our consciousness as we become more aware of Divine and Eternal Laws. As a result, we should become better people and express a higher quality in our daily lives. I cannot rate the value of this knowledge too highly. Yet it is not included in our educational curricula.

From my point of view, I have always envisaged education as a system for training children so that they can become better citizens in the human family and have opportunities for developing their individual talents under wise guidance. I now find that this important knowledge is not taught in our schools. The supreme fact that man is a spiritual being functioning temporarily through a physical body is not taught. Children are not taught that the mind is the tool of the thinker and that it can function separately from the brain which, being physical, disintegrates with the physical body.

My experiences in working for the C.F.P.S.S. have confirmed without doubt that it is an educational body meeting a need which is not being met by the Church nor by our Educational System. At Head Office, we received a steady flow of enquiries and requests for literature every day — some of these coming from clergymen and teachers — but the majority coming from the "man-in-the-street".

The numbers of lectures and articles published by the Fellowship steadily rose to meet this need, and when the Fellowship

Book Club was formed, manuscripts were accepted and books were published.

During the period when I was General Secretary, the book which had the greatest impact was *Testimony of Light* by Helen Greaves. A typical reaction is shown in the following extracts from a letter written by a Methodist minister in South Africa. He wrote:

> I have been strangely moved by the *Testimony of Light* by Helen Greaves . . . I have no recollection of ordering it But I thank God for it . . .
>
> What appealed to me was its quality and depth. My own spirit seemed to confirm the truth of what I was reading. It was a green light all the way.

Many people, after reading *Testimony of Light,* wrote for a personal copy or in order to obtain copies for relations or friends.

The Fellowship was fortunate in having the support of Helen Greaves who was blessed with psychic gifts but was not a professional medium. She had already recounted her psychic experiences in *The Dissolving Veil. Testimony of Light* was written as a result of her close association with Frances Banks who died in 1965. Frances Banks was known to many of us in the Fellowship as she was the Leader of our Committee on Mysticism. For twenty-five years she was a Sister in the Anglican Community of the Resurrection in South Africa and, during much of that time, she was Principal of the Teachers' Training College in Grahamstown. She was the author of several books on psychology and taught for some years in Maidstone Gaol. *Testimony of Light* contains communications from Frances Banks after her death which were received telepathically by Helen Greaves. In his Foreword to the book, Col. Lester wrote:

> Those of us who know both Helen Greaves and Frances Banks so well, are impressed by the authenticity of these scripts. The phrasing and content of the communications are so typical of Frances, and completely unlike the style of writing as shown by the "author" in her previous books and articles.

Dr. Robert Crookall, B.Sc. (Psychology), D.Sc., Ph.D., proved to be a prodigious psychic researcher and author of books on the subject. One of these was *The Jung-Jaffé View of Out-of-the-Body Experiences* which was published by the Fellowship. He quotes Jung as saying:

> I am convinced that the exploration of the psyche is the science of the future. Psychology . . . is only at the beginning of its development. But it is the science we need most for . . . it is not starvation, earthquakes, microbes or cancer but man himself who is man's greatest danger.

Another important book published by the Fellowship was *Nothing to Hide* by the Rev. Leonard Argyle, B.D., Hon. C.F. Having an expert knowledge of Hebrew, he shows that the well-known prohibition contained in Deuteronomy XVIII has been mistranslated. In his Introduction to the book, the Rev. D. J. Bretherton writes:

> The author brings a lifetime of study to his theme. His is the authority of an expert Hebraist who has turned years of careful investigation to good account. His historical sketch showing how the Deuteronomic passage was mis-translated and never corrected over the years is in itself an example of painstaking research and a major contribution to our knowledge of the Bible. His view that Deuteronomy 18:12 represents a condemnation of *false and fraudulent* mediumship is, to my mind, a correct evaluation which throws a completely new light on our understanding of the passage. His argument is clear, logical and convincing.

Another book published by the Fellowship should be mentioned as it refers to the Celtic Church. It is *The Celtic Church Speaks Today* by the Rev. A. W. Jackson and it records communications received from monks of the Priory of Lindisfarne through the trance mediumship of a choir boy. Relevant passages are:

> Is there among you a set festival in remembrance of Cuthbert?
>
> Not in your sense. You do understand by this time, surely, that Cuthbert lives as our over-Prior. We do not think of him quite as you do of departed saints. Frequently, thanksgiving is made for his work and the work of others with him.
>
> I suppose he is one of the "Higher Ones"?

If you like, yes. With Aidan of Iona *and Joseph of Glastonbury,* he makes up the "Monastery Triangle" who from a higher plane, rule all Celtic houses.

On another occasion I asked the communicator to tell us something about the services at the Priory, and he confirmed and amplified much information which I had already received through other channels. The form of service is not unlike that of an Anglican Cathedral, where ceremonial is fairly developed, but there are differences distinctive of the Celtic Church. Numerous religious houses all over the country actively maintain the tradition of Lindisfarne, Iona and primitive Glastonbury in earth life, *and feel themselves to possess a purer type of Christianity than the Roman Catholic Church with whom, in earth, they were in strong rivalry.*

I know, we all know, that they are truth-telling spirits, men of the highest honour and integrity who, in years of intercourse closer and closer, and more intimate than many earthly friends, have never once deceived us or evaded a plain issue. Moreover, they are educated men with a definitely progressive and critical spirit. They are impatient of legend and pious exaggerations of the devout. *They discount the Venerable Bede,* and subject to much criticism the miraculous stories of the Saints.

The formation of a Schools Speakers' Panel was an important event in the development of the Fellowship. It is significant that, when offers of speakers were sent to 212 headmasters of schools in the Midlands, 53 of the headmasters approached accepted the offer. It seemed to me that the response of 25% revealed a serious weakness in our educational system. As time went on, the work of the speakers visiting schools increased. Public Schools were included in the project and visits were also made to universities. I felt it my duty to inform the Minister for Education at that time, Mrs. Margaret Thatcher, of the way in which the Fellowship was meeting this need.

As I took part in some of the visits to schools as well as receiving requests for help because some children were carrying out experiments with ouija boards, I became increasingly aware of the need in the field of education. One of our members, who was the Principal of a Teachers' Training College, arranged a special weekend conference for students and staff which proved very successful.

In addition to publishing literature, the regular holding of branch meetings, discussion groups and annual regional conferences gave opportunities for members to increase their knowledge. Speakers on various aspects of psychical research were visiting small groups connected with churches and other groups such as Toc H., Young Conservatives, Women's Institutes, Townswomen's Guilds, etc. There was no doubt in my mind that this aspect of the work of the Fellowship was basically educational and that it had developed naturally because of imperfections in our educational system and the Theological Training Colleges. *To the man-in-the-street, this state of affairs must raise some doubts concerning the degree to which we can trust scholars and theologians to give us the right lead!*

During a period of interest in psychical research for over thirty years, I found it impossible to ignore the steady growth in the practise of spiritual healing. It seems extraordinary that the general public were kept in ignorance of this fact due, no doubt, to the extreme cautiousness of doctors, clergymen, the press, radio and television concerning psychic matters, the possibility of fraud and the strong link with Spiritualism. My own attitude was a simple one and could be summed up by the direct question, "Is spiritual healing of benefit to man?" I soon discovered that the direct answer was "Yes" but, naturally, this was qualified by the need for a responsible approach to the subject with a recognition of the need for complete co-ordination with medical skill.

Over the years, despite the climate of opinion which generally lacked interest or encouragement from the Church and medicine, the practise of the laying-on-of-hands outside the Church has steadily grown. One may well wonder how anyone begins this kind of mission. Some people, like the young lady in Vienna, undergo a direct personal experience which reveals that they can be used as a channel for the Divine healing power. Then, after seeking guidance from an unofficial body like the Fellowship, they carry out their mission as opportunities occur in their daily lives. Others may have been told by a medium that they could be used in this way. They then read about the subject, perhaps joined a local Healing Group and were encouraged to build up confidence by assisting other healers. So much healing of this kind is based on faith, yet it is mainly carried on outside the Church, that it is a constant source of astonishment to me that more church members do not appear to have as much faith in this direction as those outside the Church. As church members are directed in their lives by sermons given in the pulpit, the responsibility for this must lie largely in our theological colleges. It is not surprising that the Rev. J. Cameron Peddie called his excellent little book on healing *The Forgotten Talent*.* A note at the beginning of this book reads:

> For more than thirty years J. Cameron Peddie was a minister in Glasgow's Gorbals where he organised Youth Clubs helped to settle group feuds, and brought help to innumerable families of various creeds and races. In 1942 he began to prepare for the ministry of healing and his influence in this field has been felt by many. Today over a hundred ministers of the Church of Scotland are following his example.

The Fellowship took an active part in the promotion of knowledge of spiritual healing. It had a Central Committee on Healing, a Sub-Committee on Mental Illness and a Medical Section. Its Chairman, Col. Lester, together with Mrs. Lester, did a great deal to promote new thought on the subject by holding services for meditation and healing in many parts of the country. In December, 1968, following a service held in a church in Bristol, the minister wrote to him as follows:

> Quite a number of those who attended your service mentioned to me the wonderful atmosphere they felt and the healing power. Several who were there stopped me in the street in the following days to say how much it had meant to them and what help they had personally received. One woman had placed her nephew's name on your healing list and a week later she received a letter saying that the family did not understand it, but there had been an amazing change in his condition. Another couple, for whom we have been working for several years, and where there seemed no hope whatsoever for their domestic troubles, wrote afterwards a letter showing a complete change of attitude which is nothing less than miraculous as you would agree if they were to go into all their past history with you.

* Fontana Books (First published 1961)

In London, the Fellowship arranged for healers to be available at the Lambeth Mission once a week. I was present on one occasion when a patient described how, during healing, she felt a power like electricity flow through the whole of her body.

In an article on "Divine Healing" which was published in *Life of Faith* in August 1970, one of the Fellowship's active members, the Rev. Arthur C. Reynolds, wrote:

> It will be realised that, about the year A.D. 315, the spiritual life of the Church waned, and one result was that the ministry of healing became less prominent than in previous years . . . However, the torch was kept alight, perhaps dimly, by such persons as Bernard of Clairvaux, Francis of Assisi, Catherine of Siena, Martin Luther and John Wesley, who preserved the early tradition of Christ's command to heal. We now can claim that there has been a renaissance of the healing ministry . . . We may be thankful to God for these developments, and pray that *not only the preaching of the Gospel but the healing of the sick, being the twofold commission of Jesus, will be fully established in this land of ours* . . . The method of healing may vary, but the purpose and the effects will be the same. God needs instruments in His churches today, as the disciples were when they were sent forth to heal the sick . . . The ideal is that every church should be a house of hope in this direction.

I know two healers, husband and wife, who carried out a quiet, dedicated ministry of healing in their home for over ten years. During this period they gave over 10,000 treatments to over 1,000 patients. The natural result has been the formation of a healing group, composed mainly of church members, which meets weekly in the centre of our town. The existence of this group, which has been brought to the attention of the local Council of Churches, will, no doubt, stimulate interest among other church members. But, surely, it seems reasonable to expect such interest in the practise of one of the spiritual gifts to be stimulated from within the Church?

Members of the Medical Section of the Fellowship met regularly to try to formulate a hypothesis to explain the phenomena of healing. Some members visited healers, obtained information concerning healing cures and endeavoured to follow up cases by studying patients' medical records wherever possible.

It was soon apparent that the work was full of difficulties and that it would take a long time to obtain tangible results. Nevertheless, the existence of such a section was a hopeful sign for the future.

In a similar way, the existence of the Institute of Religion and Medicine, with its office in London and its Field Groups throughout the country, is also a hopeful sign as it affords opportunities for doctors and priests to exchange ideas at group meetings and conferences on matters of common interest.

When one of the active members of the Medical Section spoke at an annual dinner of the Home Counties Association of Spiritual Healers in January, 1970, he gave a historical survey showing how, originally, the functions of priest and healer were fused in the same individual. In time, however, the power of healing gradually dwindled and became supplanted by the spread of materialist medicine. In the 13th century, Pope Innocent III condemned surgery and all priests who practised it.

The speaker regarded the emergence of non-physical methods of healing as one of the most remarkable features of the present scene. Never before had so many people sought healing advice outside the medical profession. Further extracts from his survey reported in *Psychic News* are: *The present emphasis on medicine as an exact science, its adulation of the specialist and all the complicated techniques and machinery at the medical profession's command, had become divorced from the healing of persons. It concerned itself solely with disease, ignored the wholeness of man and denied his essential spiritual nature.*

In the name of science it had closed its eyes to all but the material body. Yet this was at a time when the most advanced scientists in other fields were rapidly becoming more convinced of the existence of an ordered scheme of being beyond physical perception.

Even religious leaders, who should know better, were not entirely free from this error. They were apt to look askance and even with apprehension at suggestions that the Church should reactivate its healing ministry.

Thinking people realised that the world's troubles today "spring entirely from the false sense of values engendered by the materialistic outlook". The situation would be dramatically changed if humanity could be convinced of the spiritual world's reality . . "The tensions of the rat race would be replaced by an ordered pattern of life in which all were working together in harmony and co-operation for the common good. This might be regarded as a heaven on earth, but of such was the kingdom of heaven. I am convinced that this is man's ultimate destiny, painfully and slowly though he evolves. Anything that helps to convince him of the reality of spiritual powers is a step forward towards that heaven. For that reason we are now witnessing the most tremendous impingement, from every possible direction, and every conceivable way of the powers of spirit on earth today".

To me, the importance of the existence of the Fellowship's Medical Section and the Institute of Religion and Medicine lies in the fact that they are composed of doctors of medicine who are concerned with man as a spiritual being. I felt it a privilege to help in the formation of the Medical Section, to watch its growth and also to attend conferences of the Institute of Religion and Medicine. These experiences left me in no doubt that a minority of doctors were becoming aware of the power of spiritual healing and that the outlook of the medical profession as a whole would eventually change. I felt it my duty to inform Sir Keith Joseph, Minister of Social Services at that time, of these events.

Once again, the theme of a spiritual lead being given by Britain in the field of spiritual healing persisted as the following experience reveals: I was visited by the minister of a church in Vermont, U.S.A. He told me that the ladies of his church had raised funds to send him to Britain to investigate spiritual healing. He joined the Fellowship immediately and attended the annual conference of the National Federation of Spiritual Healers. Just before his return to the U.S.A., he called again and told me that, as a result of his experiences, he intended introducing services for healing in his church. His interest in the subject was maintained as he visited us again the following year.

In 1970, the Academy of Parapsychology and Medicine, subtitled the Unity of Body, Mind and Spirit in Healing, was founded in California, U.S.A. Its Statement of Philosophy and Purpose includes the following:

The Academy holds certain beliefs to be axiomatic. It is believed:

That medicine must adopt a new view of man: one which recognizes the unity of body, mind and spirit and the importance of the interrelationship of these dimensions in health and disease.

That treatment of disease (in the full sense) must be directed at the whole man, and that lasting healing cannot be achieved where the mental, emotional and spiritual elements have been left untouched.

It is the conviction of the Academy that the marriage of religion and science can bring meaning to the words spoken by Plato 2300 years ago: ". . . if the head and body are to be well, you must begin by curing the soul".

Readers will remember that, in Part I, I referred to cases of interference or possession by ignorant spirits. As I write Part II of this book I am extremely conscious of the prevailing ignorance of this aspect of mental illness and the lack of official recognition of its existence.

The Fellowship's Sub-Committee on Mental Illness included a psychiatrist, a chaplain to a mental hospital, a psychiatric social worker and others who were facing up to this problem. Requests for help were received regularly at the Fellowship's Head Office and our Vice-Chairman spent much time giving practical assistance to sufferers. In addition, some of the requests for help received by a well-known psychic newspaper are forwarded to me, presumably because there are very few people in Britain who are prepared to give help in these cases. There is still a great need for the Church and Medicine to face up to this problem which many people believe is likely to get worse.

Another interesting aspect of the work of the Fellowship was the existence of its Committee on Scientific Research whose members were concerned with examining psychical research in the light of scientific progress. One of its members had held a high rank in the Department of Education and Science and it had the support of well-known experts in various fields of science as consultants. One of these consultants was Sir Alister Hardy, Fellow of the Royal Society and Emeritus Professor of Zoology at Oxford who set up a Religious Experience Research

Unit at Oxford. When interviewed by Peter Lewis of the *Daily Mail* in July 1971, he said:

> I am very well aware that some people think this is a senile whim but, in fact, I have been aiming towards it in all my work as an ecologist. *I believe that religious experience is part of our species, a power on which primitive man could draw and it must be part of any true science of man. It might also lead to a more vital and dynamic religious faith than one which rests mainly on dogmas from the past. Religion, as Dean Inge said, is concerned with that which is and not that which was.*

Up to the time of the interview by Peter Lewis, Sir Alister had collected 1,700 specimens of religious experience. His objective was 5,000. He said, "Science cannot analyse the essence of religious experience, but if we collect a large enough number of records of it, analyse them and compare them systematically, patterns may begin to emerge. In this way, we could build up a new natural history of religion".

Readers of the *Daily Mail* were invited to send details of their religious experiences to Sir Alister with the result that he received more than 600 within a few days. Peter Lewis wrote:

> They have come from people of all ages from 14 to 96 from doctors and butchers, policemen and nurses, housewives and soldiers. And they are still coming in.
>
> Some have told of dramatic or psychical events or occasions when they seemed to be possessed of a super-human power like the woman who was cycling home along a country road when she suddenly became convinced that all was not well with her child at home. "I was coming to a long hill where normally I have to get off and walk for a long while", she says "As I came to it I prayed fervently to God to help me get home quickly. To my amazement the bicycle seemed to rise off the ground. The pedals seemed to be being turned for me. With no effort I found myself at the top of the hill. I am convinced I was riding through the air, not in contact with the road at all".
>
> Another reader wrote:
>
> At 17, when I felt the world was unfair and people un-

reliable, I prayed that if God existed he would show me some sort of light in the jungle.

I was suddenly overcome, overwhelmed, saturated — no word is adequate — with a sense of sublime and living love. I was sweeping the stairs and the brush in my hand, the dustpan, the stairs, seemed to come alive with love.

I seemed to be part of this power, so wonderful that I felt I knew what the saints had grasped. It can only have been a minute or two, yet it seemed eternity.

Perhaps half a dozen times in my life I have been conscious of "the peace of God which passes all understanding'. It is a moment when one realises one's place in the universe, the loving power which holds one, a complete absence of fear and worry and a great sense of joy.

These examples reveal the value of Sir Alister's work and I hope that readers who have had psychic experiences will support these efforts which will help to bridge the gulf between religion and science.

Some years ago, the Rev. Canon J. D. Pearce-Higgins wrote the following passage in his pamphlet, *Religion, Science and the Supernormal*.

The Fellowship is open to criticism from within the Church — not only from the clergy but the laity also — who in a great number of cases do not want to be shaken out of their present way of thinking and the acceptance of facts demonstrated by psychical research usually means turning many of their cherished beliefs upside down.

We are also criticised by scientists because they prefer that their work should not be mixed up with religious ideas, believing (in most cases) that there is no obligation on their part to enter the religious field. They also say that psychical research is not truly scientific because it is incapable of guaranteed repetition. They forget, of course, that they are not dealing with matter but with human beings, with all their mental, physical and psychological idiosyncrasies. They are often unwilling to recognise that so much work has been done in this field over the past 60 or 70 years that psychical research is now worthy to take its place with the other empirical sciences.

I remember receiving letters from a young man who wished to spend his full time in psychical research. Eventually, with the help of the secretary of the Fellowship's Committee on Scientific Research, he gained a place as a student in parapsychology at Cambridge University. At that time, the committee was paying some attention to the phenomena known as "Raudive Voices" and the student devoted his preliminary studies to this phenomena. His first report, submitted in October 1970, contained the following comments:

> This phenomena was apparently discovered by Dr. Friedrich Jurgenson, who was recording bird songs and, on playing back his tapes, found that faint voices were recorded on them as well. He wrote a book about this experience; Dr. Konstantin Raudive read it and subsequently met him and witnessed a demonstration of the phenomenon. This so impressed Dr. Raudive that he embarked on his course of research and during three years of patient and careful work he recorded some 72,000 voice phenomena. In this work he has been assisted by physicists, electronic experts and parasychologists in many countries, and in 1968 he published a book (*Unhorbares Wird Horbar* — The Inaudible becomes Audible) about his findings. This book has been translated into English and will be published * within the next few months . . .
>
> The voices recorded by Dr. Raudive are very faint and difficult to distinguish from the background noise. Tapes thought to be blank have later been found to contain voice phases. According to Dr. Raudive it may take up to three months to train the ear to detect them. The most unique feature of the voice phrases is their "polyglot" composition. Even short sentences are made up of words from several languages, put together so that the whole makes sense, although the grammar leaves something to be desired. It is interesting to note that the languages used, Swedish, German, Russian, Latvian, Spanish, French and English, are all to some degree within Dr. Raudive's compass. A related characteristic is the rhythmic quality of the words, which dominates the construction of the sentences, words being compressed, arbitrarily shortened or used with ungrammatical

* Colin Smythe.

endings to conform to it. Many of the short sentences or phrases collected are trivial, inconsequential or nonsensical Often they express mundane desires or resemble the rambling words of a delirious patient. Others, however, have convinced Dr. Raudive that it is he that is being addressed (often by his nickname, Kosti), that he can identify some of the speakers and that he has been informed correctly of matter unknown to him . . .

During this period, the student was able to meet Dr. Raudive whom he described as a writer, psychologist and parapsychologist who had studied post-mortem manifestations for twenty-five years. The student also attended a conference on "World, Man and Science Tomorrow" in Austria at which papers were read on social problems, psychology, modern physics and molecular biology. In addition, an afternoon session was devoted to the voice phenomena during which four papers were presented by Dr. Raudive, an electronics expert from St. Gallen, Switzerland, a high-frequency engineer from Ulm and an electronics engineer from Vienna.

This is only one example of the work of the Fellowship's Committee on Scientific Research but it should be sufficient to reveal the value of the existence of this small group and to point to possibilities for a solid contribution to the extension of man's knowledge about himself.

III

GLASTONBURY, MYSTICISM AND LIGHT

In view of the particular place of Glastonbury in our British history, the reader may wonder if its spiritual association has been maintained and whether there are any significant occurrences taking place there today. In September, 1964, a group of people from various parts of the country met at Glastonbury. Many of them had psychic gifts and recorded their reactions which were published by a group known as The Universal Link.

One lady, who was a member of the Fellowship and known to me, recorded the following experience:

> I was told that I was to be in the Abbey grounds between six and seven o'clock to go to the Joseph of Arimathea chapel.
>
> About five-thirty, Dorothy G. and I found ourselves leaving, we were not hurrying but urgently walking along. Then the whole experience started and, never in all the most wonderful subjective and spiritual experiences which I have been privileged to have, have I known anything like this: it was quite extraordinarily vivid and so much more real than this everyday seemingly real world.
>
> As we walked through the town we suddenly became filled with a sense of urgency, and simultaneously I became aware of a great shining light in front of us and I was filled with tremendous force — felt almost to the degree of seeing. A vast multitude followed us, we were marching ahead of hundreds of thousands of people. It was so vivid and real that the town, the traffic and the people seemed to be unreal. As I registered this I turned to Dorothy in astonishment because it had happened so suddenly — to find that Dorothy was simultaneously turning to me in astonishment; we had registered exactly the same thing at the same time, but she

with her clearer vision had seen that the light ahead of us was a knight in shining armour. Again later, five minutes from the Abbey, we turned to each other both aware of the same thing happening — and this was a sense of great force rushing over our heads and into the Abbey, and I knew that it was the angelic host force. Dorothy also felt this and said, "There is a host of the angelic awaiting us in the Abbey".

We could not speak for the power was so terrific. Then we went into the Abbey and I said, "I must go straight down into the Chapel". Dorothy looked at me half-laughing and replied, "Well you cannot do anything else, the knight in armour has gone down there ahead of you". By this time I was not seeing anything, I was just caught up in this tremendous power . . . I went down the steps, walked towards the little altar at the end, took off my shoes and stood there with this enormous power about me, and I wondered what it was that was going to happen.

I do not see in a clairvoyant way, it is simply an awareness, a perception of things unseen, but in this manner they can be extremely vivid. First I became aware of a wonderful being with a long beard and a lovely multi-coloured robe, whom I instantly knew to be Joseph of Arimathea. He came forward and spoke to me, telling me that once before in another age that had then been new he had sent me out on a mission, and again in this new age he was doing the same. Then he faded from view and I saw a brilliant white light; I knew it was a figure although there was no defining form. It held towards me a beautifully shaped large shallow bowl, white and gleaming, translucent, almost like alabaster. My hands seemed to come out to take this, though they were literally nothing but vibrating force at this time, and I held it, and there was some completely wordless and quite wonderful communion. I began to feel that I was no longer anything to do with myself — I became some small, slender, pure little being who spoke to this person and called him the beloved of her heart. There seemed to be some glorious tie between these two. There was very little left of me even to be the watcher in all this, and I find it extremely difficult to put any of it into words, but please realise that behind these words lies all the beauty that was there in this happening.

The glorious figure of light faded and there were many. He was there but there were many in robes and even some in armour. I felt completely and utterly radiant, almost under a spell, my hands were crossed upon my breast and I walked in the purity and radiance of this lovely slender little being to Dorothy and called to her to come down. She told me afterwards that she did not recognize me for she saw this small radiant being herself.

She took off her shoes and we stood together where I had stood before, and she received wonderful words; we became aware also of the drama of these tremendous happenings that we were watching. Then over our heads I sensed, and so did Dorothy, the wings of a great angel whom I knew to be Gabriel. I then became aware that I had taken on the part of Mary for this drama. I wondered, with the little bit of me that was left, why this was, for it must have had some extremely strong meaning; but I did not take it personally for these things are never meant personally.

Gradually, all this faded away, though we stood for a while in awe of the sheer beauty of it all, then our hands fell to our sides — we had had our eyes shut but we both had our hands reaching out towards it instinctively. We thought it was all over; then Dorothy said she received the words, "Take her to my own bit of my original wall". As she told me this I knew at once that the one who had spoken these words was Joseph of Arimathea.

These are short extracts from a report of thirty-one pages but I chose them because I knew the two ladies concerned and can vouch for their integrity.

Another member of the group whom I knew personally and for whom I have great respect was Kathleen F. who wrote:

Nothing was outwardly arranged by us — we had no very precise instructions. Some of us had a directive to be there on a certain date, but to most of us it was an inner conviction, an impression which was too strong to resist . . . Something had called to us, something outside ourselves, and all, without any hesitation whatsoever, obeyed. We were needed in Glastonbury . . .

Glastonbury always seems to have an immense golden

movement as though a pulsing light was beating through it. Everywhere I was conscious of space in which to breathe, of peace, rest and expansion; it is indeed well named one of the secret (sacred) places of the Lord. As I gazed upon the sunlit valley it brought back a rush of memory and vivid recollection of those other days that almost seemed a part of the present as old scenes were re-enacted during that pregnant week. Here indeed was what, for want of a better word, we call power — Angelic outpouring, God vibration. It was everywhere, it was transcendental, it was under the earth, above the earth, quiet, restrained, gentle, golden — no words really can describe it, it is the wordless sound of love . . .

Sometimes during the evenings we would meet together to hear different tape-recordings given by members of other groups, and then sit in silence, tuning in on other levels. Getting insight into ourselves, our work and our meetings. These silences were charged with the power, they drew us closer together, they nourished us and we were inwardly refreshed. In the silences we slipped out of the confusion, and away from material thinking, into states of consciousness beyond the sound barrier — out of time into the eternal now — our spirits walked free in Glastonbury with those others who had freed themselves long, long ago and we pooled our experiences and so enriched each other's lives.

Everything was so natural, so spontaneous. Each served the whole, the whole served each, and always we were conscious of our unseen companions . . .

Some of us were soon conscious of a great presence — power gathered around us, enfolding us, and I became aware of the Master. He was standing in front of me, holding his hands before my eyes, those same strong beautiful hands I had seen before. Then quite clearly I heard these words, "I did my carpentering in this area" . . .

This enactment passed and I was aware of the walls of the room disappearing and I was looking straight down into a sunlit valley gazing at a man coming up the slope towards me. *His image is etched in my mind for all time.* He walked with long easy strides, his bare head thrown back, his arms extended in a gesture of freedom and love. The sleeves of his loose cloak fell in soft folds from the outstretched arms, and he was wearing a white undergarment of a very fine material. The cloak looked very dark, but I couldn't tell the colour. *But what really held me spell-bound was the fact that I was looking at the eternal spirit of perfection. Here was perfect symmetry, moral fibre and spiritual attainment — never have I seen flesh and spirit so one, so knit together, so glowing, so alive.* He was followed by a group of white-robed people, stretched out as a company of companions and not moving in a single file. He walked as their leader with great purpose, as though towards a particular goal.

In 1971, I received further news of Kathleen F. who reported a visit to Switzerland in connection with a group called World Harmony. An extract from the report reads:

Travelling almost daily from light centre to light centre our particular function seemed to be that of linking the so-called past with the ever present. There were reservoirs of light to be tapped with all the great abbeys and churches. With deep intent we directed this same divine flow towards universal world harmony and our own and humanity's need for an increasing awareness of God's consciousness. Fusing all aspects of light with the One Light.

We prayed in the Abbey of the Black Virgin at Einsiedeln, visited Warden House where Nicholas, the patron saint of Switzerland lived with his family, before he was led to go into retreat nearby. We met the head Lama in the new Tibetan Centre, and one dripping wet Sunday evening in Vevey we joined with at least one hundred and fifty people in an ecumenical "March of Unity", sharing in the services held in the Roman Catholic Church, the Protestant Church, the Russian Orthodox Church, etc., realising vividly that we were people of the ONE and not separate congregations.

I think the strongest impression I had of the links that I was so privileged to meet was that of their "inner knowing". There was a directness and an earnestness, an approach of clear seeing that gave them strength and purpose in what they said and did.

Following the visit to Switzerland, Kathleen F. was travelling to America. In view of her experiences at Glastonbury, I was intrigued by her reference to the work of the group in linking the so-called past with the ever present. This is yet another example of inspired action stemming from Britain.

When writing of happenings related to Glastonbury in the seventies, it is essential that I should include a reference to a body of people known as the Companions and Friends of Chalice Well, Glastonbury, which was formed by Major W. Tudor Pole. Major Tudor Pole was regarded by many people as a modern seer. In his annual message to members in 1966, he wrote:

> When we met a year ago, I said a few words about Britain's destiny and the role our Island people could fulfil in the years to come. Britain and her people are now passing through a valley of deep humiliation. The Empire that stretched across the globe and ruled the seas is no more. The Commonwealth which took its place is already fragmented and internally divided almost beyond repair. Two world wars have drained our resources to such an extent that we seem unable even to pay our way. Politically and economically Britain has ceased to be a world power and even as an intermediary between East and West her influence is becoming negligible. What is left? Is Britain's Destiny to follow in the footsteps of the Decline and Fall of the Roman and earlier Empires? On the other hand can an important purpose lie behind our present humiliation and our loss of influence within the Council of Nations? Yes. I think there can be such a purpose and I will tell you why?
>
> In my view there is a certain basic stability of character in our Island stock, in spite of the frivolities and selfishness caused by the present wave of material but illusive affluence. As individuals, speaking in general terms, we are still too insular in outlook, too sure that, by Divine intent, we are superior in character and intelligence to other people and other races. We still regard Europeans as "foreigners", Americans as adolescents and Easterners as belonging to an inferior breed. There are, of course, many individual exceptions to these generalities but, in the main, are they not a fair picture of our attitude towards the rest of the world and its inhabitants? It can well be that one of the main purposes behind our present humiliation is to bring about a

change of mind and heart. In this way, we could become equipped to fulfil the role of a Servant Nation in world affairs, one that would be far more valuable in potential achievement than could be realised in any other way. At present, the human race is in urgent need of leadership that would lift it out of the present darkness into the light of a new Day.

We are living in a time of world tensions and tribulations. It is all too easy to reflect these conditions in our daily lives, and in this way to increase the general confusion and anxiety. But let us look up and look forward. True leadership need not depend upon wealth and power of the material kind but it does call for humility, courage, vision and strong determination. *I see no good reason why we should not be able to use our present tribulations as a stepping stone towards the mission of becoming a people capable of throwing up leaders of spiritual capacity and world wide vision. This great opportunity is ours to grasp if we can be sufficiently modest and perceptive to do so.*

Where better than Chalice Well to sow the seeds of such a purpose and to tend them carefully, under the guidance of the "Revealer of the Word" whose unseen presence is already in our midst?

As members of the Fellowship became more interested in meditation, its title was extended to include "Spiritual" studies and a Committee on Mysticism was formed. Until I became more closely involved with the work of the Fellowship, I had little knowledge of the Mystics and the word "mysticism" had little meaning for me.

In his book *Mysticism,** F. C. Happold wrote:

The word "mystic" has its origin in the Greek mysteries. A mystic was one who had been initiated into these mysteries, through which he had gained an esoteric knowledge of divine things and been "reborn into eternity". His object was to break through the world of history and time into that of eternity and timelessness . . . Through the mysteries, the initiated entered into something holy and numinous, a secret wisdom about which it was unlawful for him to speak . . .

* Pelican Books.

> Mysticism has its fount in what is the raw material of all religion and is also the inspiration of much of philosophy, poetry, art and music, a consciousness of a *beyond,* of something which, though it is interwoven with it, is not of the external world of material phenomena, of an *unseen* over and above the seen. In the developed mystic this consciousness is present in an intense and highly specialised form . . . *In the true mystic there is a release of latent powers and a widening of vision, so that aspects of truth unplumbed by the rational intellect are revealed to him . . . In the religious mystic there is a direct experience of the Presence of God. Though he may not be able to describe it in words, though he may not be able logically to demonstrate its validity, to the mystic his experience is fully and absolutely valid and is surrounded with complete certainty.*

In his book, Mr. Happold surveyed mysticism in India, Palestine and Greece and then wrote about the Christian Revelation as follows:

> At the time of the birth of Christ, the Mediterranean world was, if not waiting, at least ripe for a new revelation. That revelation came in Jesus Christ. The contact of Jesus with his disciples was an experience of so compelling a character that it impelled them to declare with complete and utter conviction that the Man who had died on the cross on Calvary had risen and was alive again. He was the Son of God. Though He had returned to the eternal world, at Pentecost the Spirit had descended on them.
>
> To their contempories it was an astonishing and incredible statement, to the Jews a stumbling block, to the Greeks foolishness . . . An inner experience of the immanence of God in man had been known in India and reflection on it had resulted in those two fundamental statements which are the glory of the Hindu faith. This inner experience was, however, unrelated to history. In consequence, Hinduism failed to find and express — though in the Gita it moves towards it — a completely satisfactory synthesis between history and non-history, between time and timelessness, between matter and spirit. *It fell to Christianity to try to find and express a richer synthesis . . .*

> *The insights of India, of Palestine and of Greece were not superseded. They were fulfilled.*

There has been a growing interest by young people in meditation and mysticism which was high-lighted by the publicity given to the interest shown by members of the pop group "The Beatles". In addition, publicity has been given to the visits of advanced yogi from India to Britain. The fact that young people have been attracted to eastern mysticism indicates a weakness in the Church which, in general, has not recognised this need and does not yet seem able to meet it.

The Fellowship's Committee on Mysticism has helped the formation of small groups for meditation and has issued explanatory literature on the subject. The following extracts are taken from the committee's first booklet, *Mysticism*:

> The discipline undertaken by the would-be mystic involves two simultaneous motions of the Will. In one he surrenders his separate identity completely "for Love's sake". In desiring to become one with God he must be willing to become one with created life of all kinds and at all levels. In turn this will mean that he becomes increasingly vulnerable, experiencing joy and pain to the limit of his capacity, almost as God does. As he is bound to suffer, with his increased sensitivity, so will his compassion grow in like measure. Surely, this is the effect which Christianity is intended to have upon us.
>
> So the little human becomes charged and surcharged in his body, heart and mind; and in time changes occur in his soul, as a result of the working of these influences. The more he exercises his spiritual faculties, the more capable they become of receiving these influences; and, once charged, he is capable of radiating their love, peace, truth, light or beauty — not only to humans, but also to other kingdoms — mineral, vegetable or animal.

In another booklet, *Meditation*, members of the committee described their personal reactions to meditation exercises. One member, a doctor of medicine, wrote:

> The inevitable result of my meditation is a feeling of mental relaxation and a renewed awareness of the very circumscribed nature of the world in which I do my daily

> work. In meditation, I am in a vast, intangible reality that far outdistances anything I know in normal consciousness. I therefore regain a sense of perspective in relation to the daily problems that beset me . . . The practice of meditation leads to the experience of serenity in my approach to the world. *The love of God becomes a reality, and love for one's fellow men also becomes real . . . Meditation is a mental hygiene which, by enabling the mind to move above material consciousness, allows it to become receptive to higher intelligences.*

This doctor became the Leader of the Committee on Mysticism and six lectures which he gave at the College of Psychic Studies were published jointly by the College and the Fellowship in a booklet called *An Approach to Mysticism.* In one lecture he said:

> It is apparent that mystical experience comes by dint of hard labour. Even those who are blessed with spontaneous extrovertive illumination will be found to have worked hard and to be advanced souls. For the experience is nothing without the change in outlook that must follow it. By this alone can the validity of the experience be judged. *At present, there is a vogue for meditation, especially in the Eastern manner, and many believe that by a simple technique they will acquire cosmic consciousness. Those with greater spiritual knowledge are not impressed. While the practise of guided meditation is a valuable technique of mind control, it will not on its own lead to illumination. This requires a life's work spent in love and ardour, in selflessness and devotion to the highest. It is on such that the Divine grace descends.*

The natural emergence of this committee again indicates, I suggest, how the work of the Fellowship is fulfilling a need which is not being met by the Church, which should meet the spiritual needs of our people.

Throughout the centuries, Christians have prayed, "Lighten our darkness, we beseech thee, O Lord" and it is not surprising that Christ is depicted as "The Light of the World" in the well-known painting which hangs in St. Paul's Cathedral. If there is indeed a spiritual awakening taking place now, one would expect to find references to Light. These are three examples which clearly show that emphasis on a new concept of Light as a concrete spiritual power is being made:

In her book *The Science of Wisdom*,* Clarice Toyne writes:

> Light has a profound effect throughout all levels of life. Focussed and effortful thought increases the energy in the brain particles. This speeds up the energy-activity in the brain cells and, as the thinker stimulates his thought to ever-increasing rates of vibration, so does the energy content of the mind increase . . . the mind which uses the brain as its physical coating. A keynote of increased energy activity is struck which magnetically allows a great inflow of like energies from the inner levels of Spirit. Intensified thought raised into the higher levels within is prayer and meditation. Hence the function of prayer and elevated thought is to flood the mind — and the brain — with more energy, with more Light. This is the Light to which all mystics testify, which is to be discovered by the ardent in prayerful concentration. He fills himself with the power of the Spirit — which is of God. This was the Light which shone on the face of Moses when he carried the tablets down from the mountain. From David, Ezekiel, Isaiah and the other prophets, the spray from the Ultimate Ocean of Truth reached the ears of their fellow-men. The Christ Light was shining through each according to his power to catch it and reflect its glory.
>
> Through the prism of Jesus the celestial Christ Ray shone upon all. Because of the perfection, the state of high attunement of the man, the Holy One could shower His beam onto the surface of life. Thus the power and the glory of that time so long ago has spread through Christendom, wherever mankind had provided a suitable ground for its blossoming. The sublime example set to the ways of man, in a perfect life lived perfectly, has inspired many to follow His way. And those who have used the inspiration of His story to seek the Kingdom within themselves, have learned how to fuse it with the Light of the Christ within.

I have already referred to the power of the communications from Frances Banks recorded in *Testimony of Light* by Helen Greaves. It is, of course, obvious that the emphasis on Light is given immediately in the title of the book.

* Sidgwick & Jackson Ltd.

When transmitting details of her discussions with a scientist on the other side, Frances said that they agreed that the scientist's attempt at changing the vibratory rate of matter is the same as the ancient teaching of the Light permeating the density of man's immersion in matter. If man could keep the Divine Light in mind, he has the power to transform those particles into a finer vibration.

She continued:

Light! How much I am learning of the meaning of that word here! How deeply I am beginning to realise the depth of those words "Light which lighteth every man that cometh into the world". How paltry is our conception of Light!

Jesus came to show and demonstrate that man lived on after leaving the earth plane. He taught that this God Force, this Life is truly within every one of us, dimmed yet unextinguishable. He was not received by His fellows, yet His Light, that High Frequency of vibration which He was able to transmit to earth, lives on . . .

I revel in Light and peace and a new joy. I cannot describe it more clearly than that. If I say that now I understand the meaning of the phrase "Rest in the Lord" that might help. Yet there is no personality about this experience. God is Light, Energy and Joy to me. I rest in the Light and am healed from my many mistakes. And I live a more abundant life.

The saying on earth "As a man thinks, so is he" is true in essence, truer than our ideas can conceive. By man's thoughts and aspirations he weaves for himself his future place in this dimension. He is known here for what he is and for what his inner subjective life has made him. Think then of the importance of Light in the soul. The intensity and power with which Light illumines the inner life are objectified here. "Lay up for yourselves treasures in heaven" may be taken as having a factual meaning . . .

Back we come to the great Truth I am imbibing more and more though, as we know, its meaning was apparent in all our teachings on earth, if only we could follow them. Light! Light! and yet more Light! Light to educate and uplift the minds of the people, bringing calmness and peace in a sure reliance of life's Purpose and the wonder of Divine Creation. Light in their souls and in their minds to lift them above the illusion of earthlife's fears. Light in their minds to teach them how to "tune in" any frustration of the life or personality to the great reality of Divine Love. Doctor X spoke of a pure Light Ray. Before this century is out he says that this method of employing Light will have become a great medical art and treatment to alleviate and arrest suffering.

You must by now be realising the tremendous importance and reality associated with Light. If you recall, we worked on earth trying to attain Light. Such experiences must be sought more positively, and with greater use of the intuitive powers, by those in the world who would wish to lift the slow vibration of the planet. More and more positively I am stretching out into the Light. By thought and by will, the realisation of Light surrounding me, interpenetrating through every stratum of my being, has become my study, my concentration and my meditation at this stage.

Freewill, the development of the logical mind, the illusions of the senses, all these tend to extinguish, or at least to dim, the Light of Divinity. Now I perceive more clearly, for I am no longer cluttered by illusions, that the great purpose of life in matter is to illumine matter with Spirit. Now, I let go. I seek for nothing. I absorb and am absorbed by the Spirit of Light, Love and Beauty. I know that I am being remade. Consciousness is expanding to acknowledge and accept the fact of being a Child of the Living Light, of already having, in consciousness, all that is needed and reflected as much as the spirit will permit.

I am free, as far as my progress will allow, and believe me the barriers are in one's own consciousness, to pursue my explorations into the nature of Eternity. The only hindrances to progress are from one's limited reception of Light. I can only liken this to the transmission of electricity. Intenser electric light and power need greater voltage; greater voltage requires thicker cables of connecting wires. One must have developed the "thicker cable" with all the leads-in united and "plugged in".

Jesus said, "I am the Light of the World" and truly He had found and could live in that Light. We are striving to live also in that Light as it presents itself as truth to us individually. This is the glory of the Christian religion.

All I realise now emphasises the reality and practicality of Jesus' teaching. Within is the Kingdom of Heaven. "Seek ye first the Kingdom of Heaven and all these things shall be added unto you". All, all was within me then, as now, but the veil of glamour and illusion barred my sight, as it still veils Reality for most dwellers on earth.

If there is any message in these writings it is the simple statement that all is Unity and that Unity is Light. We are progressing into Light and yet more Light. Light here is literally the substance and matter of our thought life. Thus, as our thoughts become attuned to the vibration of Creative Divinity, so the substance of our bodies changes, becomes less dense and reflecting more Light. We carry our own Light. The greater therefore the selflessness and illumination of our minds and the more positive our response to the higher vibration, the purer and brighter is the Light transmitted by us. "Let your Light so shine before men . . ." is essentially a fact here where each is revealed by his Light.

The third example is taken from an experience which came my way unexpectedly. I did not seek it. A few years ago, after speaking to the Cheltenham branch of the Fellowship, I stayed overnight with a daughter of Sir Oliver Lodge. During a chat at breakfast the following morning, she asked me if I had read the book, *Armour of Light* * by Olive C. B. Pixley. I had not read the book so I made a note of it. However, some months went by without my obtaining a copy. Then, on visiting Oxford for a meeting, I was told more about the book. This event led me to follow it up and read about the fascinating events in the life of Olive Pixley. Like Grace Rosher, she had had no interest in psychic matters but the sudden death of her brother, with whom she had a strong telepathic link, triggered off a sequence of important happenings.

Firstly, she found that her brother could communicate directly with her. One of the things he asked her to do was to arrange a memorial service for him at St. Martins-in-the-Fields, London as he said the prayers from the service would help him.

Secondly, she developed a power so that, when she visited ancient sites in Britain such as Avebury, Stonehenge, tors on

* Helios Book Service Ltd.

Dartmoor and Winchester, she was able to "tune in" to past events in their histories. She was also able to receive in conscious vision the ritual of the ancient worships of the true Light. That meant going throught the experiences of both priest and neophyte of the Egyptian, Hermetic and Mithraic initiations.

Finally, she was trained in the Christian initiation and was given exercises in the visualisation of Light which are recorded in the book, *The Armour of Light.* In her introduction to the book, she wrote:

> Finally, I was started on the Christian Initiation. It is difficult to remember now those early stepping stones of revelation, when the action of the cosmic rays of matter was made clear to me. I knew then why it had taken Jesus thirty years to perfect His humanity. Step by step I was made aware of the power of the blood. I was shown how humanity had polluted its bloodstream by fear, greed, cruelty and worry, and that it could be regenerated only if some great entity, who had never fallen at the Adamic crisis, would voluntarily take on that contaminated condition, and by utter selflessness, fearlessness and love, purify it. This Jesus did, and His purified blood has become available for the whole world to contact . . .
>
> The health receiving Technique in Light can be universal and is in line with the scientific discoveries of our day . . . The prophets of the Old Testament were connected with cosmic sound wavelengths . . . Christ calls and needs us, for He cannot work without us. Some of us respond; some of us do not. He cannot force us . . . Self-indulgence and self-pity are corroding conditions, and insulate one's receptivity . . . We must teach the young that they have a television set in their head and that God has a daily programme for them . . .
>
> Do realise that by putting on your inside armour of Light every day you become a child of Light . . .
>
> The general purpose of the Technique is the complete reconstruction of the self, including the actual substance of the physical body. The self, when transformed, becomes a channel for the transmission of new life to all living creatures, and of new radiations to the very earth itself. Though we speak of it as new, it is actually a return to the state enjoyed

by humanity before the Fall. At the Fall man chose to cut his direct link with divine energy and so to corrupt his own substance, and upset the entire equilibrium of the earth planet. The essence of the redemption which Jesus Christ accomplished for us was the restoration of this link, and His teaching, when fully manifested on this earth, will give us back all the powers we originally had. The Technique is a means of bringing about in Christians this complete manifestation, which has never been demonstrated in full since the days of the early Church. It never can be demonstrated unless and until a group of ordinary people like ourselves will make its demonstration their conscious aim.

The method of acquiring this new experience is to draw from God, its source, through Christ its only mediator, a new quality of life energy, and each exercise brings some measure of this increased energy to the self. The result is a self transmuted, freed from its fears and inhibitions, immune to disease, and able to transmit healing and freedom to those with whom it comes in contact . . .

We are the instruments by which this supreme and superb life energy is to be earthed and transmuted. We are the receptive end of the process, and our function is to receive and transmit the radiant life of God in each sparkling moment of which life is composed. By so doing we form within ourselves a new and glorified substance, and in transmitting it we help greatly to uplift and redeem humanity and the world.

These examples reveal, I suggest, that Divine Revelation is continuous. They also reveal to some degree how it works — from the wisdom above to those on earth who are sufficiently sensitive to respond to these subtle influences. At the same time, I realise that they are only my examples from experiences in my life and that they must also be happening to many other people.

Concerning Olive Pixley's revelation, I had been having a chat with our rector one Saturday morning during which I referred to my belief in a timing in events and guidance in our daily lives. In order to illustrate these beliefs, I told him how my attention had been drawn to the book *The Armour of Light*. He tended to "pooh-pooh" the idea but this event had an interesting sequel. At the time of our chat, I had no recollection of the relationship of the following day, Sunday, to the Church Calendar. The next morning, I discovered that it was the First Sunday in Advent which is the first Sunday in the church year. Furthermore, I found that the Collect for the day contained the following passage:

> Almighty God, give us grace that we may cast away the works of darkness and put upon us *the armour of light.*

In addition, the Epistle for the day contained the following extract from Romans VIII: 8:

> The night is far spent, the day is at hand; let us therefore cast off the works of darkness and let us put on *the armour of light.*

IV

DIVINE LAWS, CRIME AND SPIRITUAL GROWTH

The average man, who is not particularly concerned with spiritual matters and whose ideas on life are governed by a sensational national press and materialistic views expressed in plays, etc., on television and radio, could accept the reports on the steady increase in crime in most parts of the world as inevitable and completely beyond his control. He may have read or heard that, in Britain, known crimes of violence against people increased from 4,800 in 1949 to 36,600 in 1969 and that violent offences against property during the same period rose from 92,000 to 427,000. He may also have read that New York has the highest murder rate in America — 1,105 in 1969 — and a crime rate double the national average. Its choking pollution, pitiful poverty, racial hostility and a crisis of municipal bankruptcy, moved the Mayor of Boston to state during a visit in 1971, "This may be the first tangible sign of the collapse of our civilisation".

On the other hand, the personal experiences and reports included in this book reveal without doubt that, *at the same time that the increase in crime and acts of violence is taking place, a great power for good is also operating to an ever stronger degree*. As a result, despite the apparent ineffectiveness of the Church, more and more people are responding to this power and counterbalancing those responding to selfish desires which find their outlet in crime. BUT this response is rarely reported to the nation because it is not sensational and is not considered to be news by those who select what one may read or hear or what should be omitted.

Furthermore, as the basic facts about survival after death are not taught our children in school, not taught by the Church nor by parents in their homes, it is not surprising that we are saddled in our sophisticated civilisation with an increasing volume of crime. In many cases, it seems that the problem is a simple one of knowledge versus ignorance. *In general, the criminal is quite unaware that, although he may commit a crime and avoid being caught by the police in this life, he can never avoid the consequences of his act which await him in the next life.*

Our ancestors, who held a simple faith, also had a vivid imagination about hell. A modern conception of hell is obtained through the study of psychical research. The following extracts contain information given by Frances Banks in *Testimony of Light.*

> I have, with Mother Florence's permission, been allowed to accompany her and some of the Sisters on their missionary work into the Shadow Lands. It is a salutory experience. I am specially being instructed to recount the sad adventure to you, that it might be included in the book. For it might be of use in clarifying the illusory ideas on the states of Heaven and Hell which have been fostered through the centuries.
>
> There are Heavens . . . I myself can vouch for the little heaven of beauty, tranquility and loving service which it has been my happy lot to contact here. But there are spheres of unimaginable joy and beauty beyond . . . building up and extending out of every state of development . . . right on, I believe, to the Spiritual Worlds of Divine Thought, far beyond any conception you and I can have of them. Such is the progress of the soul towards these Spheres of Perfection and it is assuring to realise that we have all Eternity in which to journey onwards and "upwards".
>
> *But there are also Hells though certainly differing from the physical hells and everlasting fiery torments of man's warped imagination. There are hells of the spirit and the mind, confining states of misery; dark, depressing and as real as the tortured consciousness of the dweller therein makes them.* Yet these hells are not eternal. The man (or woman) in these mental torments need stay there no longer than his desires keep him. He is free to resist the hatreds, cruelties, lusts of his lower nature which he has retained from his earth life and which are keeping him in dark

dungeons amid like-minded inhabitants. He can always choose to follow the Light of Love, Forgiveness and Harmony and always there are souls ready to help, to guide, to comfort and to assist.

No soul is ever left comfortless unless he wishes it.

That sounds like a paradox, but then much that we learn here is very different from the teaching of many, even good men who are limited in their ideas. Existence on earth is a state of living in a thought world, illusory, and much restricted and enclosed by the glamorous web of matter. Beyond physical death the thought world is more apparent and certainly far more potent in its effects. Cause and Effect is still the Law on this plane of astral matter, as it is on earth. I understand that only as the soul proceeds onward in its progress into Higher Realms can this Law be superseded, and then other and higher Laws must be obeyed. But to my mission.

Mother Florence, two other Sisters and I, made our journey into what you would call the Underworld. Here we prefer the description Shadow Land, for this is indeed a Land of Shadows. The journey to this place is difficult and wearying for we have, by concentrated thought power, to "slow down" our vibrations so that our "bodies" will be able to endure the physical conditions pertaining therein. The Sisters never go without the special Messengers who guide them there and conduct them to the various stations on the way.

The Shadow Land is a very real place indeed; a gloomy murk covers it to which one has to become accustomed; squalid dwellings inhabited by unhappy, tormented beings who jeer and mock and pursue their warped existences. Sometimes these poor souls live in hatred and rebellion, sometimes in apathy and sometimes in a fierce denial that there is any other state of existence possible.

Frances describes the condition of a man who had been a well-known and extremely powerful Nazi leader during the last war. For twenty earth years he had been "wandering in the lower places", imprisoned by his own evil. He had been rescued, was conscious of his terrible cruelty and filled with remorse. The missionary band was told that he had come to be healed and to be enabled to face himself and judge his deeds when he wakened from his terrible ordeal of darkness. She wrote:

> The ward was dark and gloomy, very different from our usual light and sunny rooms. A pall of murky twilight seemed to hover over it. Only slowly did it become apparent to us that "something" lay on the bed. I looked away quickly from the repellent sight. The poor creature's body appeared to be covered with sores and scars; the eyes were closed The man was a terrible and pathetic sight.

Commenting on the process of personal judgment she wrote:

> There is no compulsion, of course, to review one's past life on earth as soon as one arrives and the new life here begins. Some take a long while to tackle the problem. They dread to see the effects of mistakes and failures. Some of our patients here have got "stuck" . . . During this experience the whole cycle of your life-term unfolds before you in a kaleidoscopic series of pictures. During this crisis one seems to be entirely alone. Yours is the judgment. You stand at your own bar of judgment. You make your own decisions. You take your own blame. You are the accused, the judge and jury.
>
> This is where quite a few souls in this Rest Home have become immobilised. Their pictures were too searing in their exposures. So we try to help them along, but only when they have made the "inner desire" to right their wrongs. Until that decision I do not know what happens to them, but should think that they are "prisoners of the self".

So here is a modern concept of Hell which must be a terrible experience for those who have carried out acts of cruelty and violence in their earthly lives. *But the stark fact is that most of them are quite unaware that this kind of Hell awaits them and that they cannot avoid this "Day of Reckoning".*

Personally, I am convinced that this problem resolves itself to one of education and that the knowledge of survival after death will prove to be a powerful ally in reducing the incidence of crime. As a result of this conviction, I wrote to the Home Secretary, Reginald Maudling, advising him of the existence and growth of the Fellowship and the possibility of its work assisting his department.

It should also be noted that, at the Annual Conference of the Samaritans in 1971, Professor Ivor Mills, Professor of Investigative Medicine at Cambridge, reported that during the previous seven years the number of attempted suicides had increased from 50,000 to 90,000 a year. The would-be suicide is under the mistaken impression that the ending of his physical life will solve his problems. In fact, he finds that he is still alive and that he has added to his problems by an irrevocable act. Surely, a greater amount of education concerning life after death would help to reduce this figure?

It will be remembered that Frances referred to the law of Cause and Effect still operating in the next world. It seems quite clear to me that we live under two sets of laws — man-made laws and eternal laws. As this life is only a minute section of eternity, it is obvious that any knowledge of eternal laws is of the utmost importance yet little attention appears to be paid to them in relation to man and daily life.

The events recorded in this book reveal that more and more people are seeking a meaning to life. As their minds reach out in a desire for Truth they gain glimpses of eternal truths and, therefore, gradually acquire more knowledge of the eternal laws. In most cases, this results in changes in their habits which allow an expression at a greater spiritual level and allow guidance to operate in their daily lives to a greater degree. They find that they meet more people with whom they feel spiritually attuned and that the contacts spark off further illumination which accelerates the rate of spiritual progress of those involved in the shared experiences.

In the booklet *An Approach to Spirituality* * Martin Israel, M.B., writes:

> In Martin Buber's concept of I-Thou relationship there is a giving in both participants, and the Spirit of God is felt between them and in them. The point is that in relating positively to another person the defences that hide one's real being are drawn back and one gives unreservedly of oneself to the other. This is a most dangerous thing to do, for it is the nature of life that the other will betray one, not necessarily because of malice but simply through ignorance of the pearl cast before him. In being naked as it were before the other, one has sacrificed all outer trappings of personality and bares

* C.F.P.S.S.

one's very soul to him. And in this great act of faith one loses one's life in order to gain eternal life. In other words, the superficial identification one has with the outer trappings of personality is shown to be illusory, for they themselves are insubstantial dross. Shorn of the mask, the soul, the being of eternal life in each one of us, lies revealed. To the other, unless he be a person of spiritual development, this means little, but to onself it is the pearl of great price revealed in the centre of one's own being. This act of self-disclosure, of offering oneself as a living sacrifice, is the heart of spirituality in life. It was the supreme act of love that Jesus showed in His passion in which He took upon Himself the sins of others uncomplainingly and unresentful, and it is this that makes His witness so powerful a confirmation of the presence of God in everyday life, redeeming the sordid and the brutal and spiritualising the gross and the unclean.

This is the height of relationships in life. In everyday life true relationship is always an act of giving, and this positively means an act of conscious will. One gives of one's attention to the other, ceasing to be enmeshed in a fabric of selfish imagining that wrongly passes for thought, and listens attentively. This listening is not only with the ears; it includes the eyes and the heart also.

It is my personal experience that this kind of spiritual upliftment is being felt by more and more people who have had no theological training and who may have no connection with the Church. Nevertheless, such experiences deepen their faith and tend to draw them back to the Church. It seems essential that the Church is prepared to accept them in a new way so that the process of spiritual progress continues with the fellowship available within the Church.

One of our greatly inspired but little known contemporary writers on spiritual values was Ian Fearn, an Anglican priest who devoted his life to discovering ways for men to live creatively and release the potential spirit. We are told that:

"When he came into the room, you instantly knew that you were confronted by a unique being".

"He illumined the whole of life — giving it purpose and meaning".

"He was a man who embraced a very wide horizon of life and human society; one who knew how to synthesise the knowledge necessary for realising the future of man".

The following extracts from his booklets *Greater Than we Know* * and *Think Again* * speak for themselves:

> Man is by no means a finished product. He is but the latest experiment in the process of evolving life. The challenge of Life today is for man to liberate his Spirit and so cultivate its power that he may grow to play a master role as maker of a new destiny.
>
> Our nature birth is just a preliminary for us to achieve a second birth — "being born again", as Christ called it. Unless we achieve that metamorphosis we miss the purpose in our coming here. For we each come for some specific purpose, and we must discover and fulfil that purpose ourselves, no God or anyone else can do it for us.
>
> When we have begun to educate the body so that it becomes less and less demanding and difficult, more refined through response to the aesthetic values of Life, then we shall be on the way of discovering that there is something deeper within us — the dynamic quality of Life resident in our Spirit. Hitherto, it has been dominated by matter and suffocated by the psyche and the emotions. None of us can know our own Spirit until, through the control of the psyche, we refine and make exquisite the body to be a vehicle through which that Spirit can work.
>
> This is a challenge to the young of all ages; for youth is not really a matter of years, rather is it an attitude that adjusts to and keeps pace with the movement of Life. The youthful in spirit are out to learn. When we cease to learn we cease to grow, and ceasing to grow we degenerate into fogeys and fossils, and such out-of-date survivals can have no place in a forward-moving civilisation.
>
> Only the progressive spirit can keep the experienced man young and the inexperienced learnable. That is the spirit that should animate us all in this day of dynamic challenge and creative opportunity.
>
> That dynamic inspiration that stirs within man is the motion of his spirit, and if he learns to recognise and follow

* New Renascence, Weald, Laughton, Lewes.

the inner prompting, it will gradually reveal to him where he belongs, whence he came and whither he must wend his way to fulfil his destiny. The Spirit of Life is always urging us onward. If we do not respond and move with it that Spirit is frustrated. Its striving within us is witness that there is something more beyond — something "towards which the whole of creation moves".

V

FULL CYCLE

It must be obvious to my reader that I have gone through phases in my life which have resulted in changes in my outlook and beliefs. Looking back, I am now aware that, during the period recorded in Part I when I was immersed in psychic matters, I was biassed in my attitudes and limited by my ignorance of the true depth and richness of Christianity. As I began to study Christianity as an adult, I was inevitably drawn back to the Church. I am now an active worker in the Church and feel that this position is right for me. At the same time, I am aware that similar phases have occurred in the lives of many people and, therefore, the record of my personal research into psychic phenomena can be of value as it expresses the reactions of one to whom the experience proved to be a revelation which was not afforded by the Church.

Concerning mediumship, I am now in complete agreement with Major W. Tudor Pole who wrote the following in an article on *Lines of Communication* published in the Summer 1968 issue of *Light* *:

> It is far from my intention to try and belittle the value of many spirit communications, linking the seen with the unseen, that continue to be received through mediumship. Such messages bring solace to the bereaved, have done and are doing, much to destroy the fear of the illusion we call death; and a number of them contain, and have contained, teachings of genuine spiritual and philosophical importance. *It is evident, however, to the discerning that the time is now ripe for the gradual upliftment of human consciousness from the level of the phenomenal communication to that of what may be termed spiritual communion.* Such a concept could well include a process which could be described as a form of metaphysical telepathy, mind meeting mind harmoniously,

* College of Psychic Studies.

quite irrespective of time, space or dimension. From time immemorial saints, initiates and many far less evolved individuals have achieved this goal through prayer, meditation and silence. For them, no second-hand lines of communication are necessary, and the risks of misinterpretation are greatly reduced. In this manner, the Christ within us awakes, and is able to act as guide and comforter forthwith.

Readers will remember that it was after listening to Sir Oliver Lodge that I commenced my personal search into psychic phenomena. Following the reference by Major Tudor Pole to the "Christ within us", it is appropriate to quote an extract from a spirit communication alleged to have been received from Sir Oliver Lodge at a seance held on the 20th April 1944 and recorded in the *Journal* of the Society for Psychical Research. He said:

> There is always that that we call, for want of a better term, the divine spark, that animates us automatically. I used to say that human beings were bits struck off the Rock of Life, and that some God might wish to be struck off, and some were struck off wantonly, but they have become human individual egos and the divine spark therefore enthroned in each piece that was struck off the Rock of Life. You can't strike a piece off, chip a piece off the Rock of Life but it has to be animated; the animation is there, in every infinitesimal piece that you strike off. Well, it is this spark which is always calling me back to God, back to the Rock, back to that from which it has sprung. It is always inciting man to do this or that or the other that they may bring his efforts in train, in harmony with that divine source from which it springs. And it does it.

The value of any knowledge must be related to the degree to which it helps us to fulfil our individual destiny in our daily lives. In this respect, providing it is kept in a reasonable perspective, I do not know of any knowledge to compare with that obtained through psychical research. In our present state, it can be an important "stepping stone" towards a deeper understanding of Christianity and the Church. Although it meets the needs of some people, and I can appreciate that the attitude of the Church was probably the cause, it seems to me to be a pity that Spiritualism became established as a religion. The motto of the Fellowship, "To Faith add Knowledge" appears to me to be a reasonable approach.

In addition, having gained a concept of the importance of our British Christian heritage since my experiences in the psychic field, my views have become strengthened. Events show that Britain is giving a strong lead in psychic matters in the seventies. If this energy is regarded as part of the continuous Divine Revelation, it seems reasonable to expect it to be moulded into the ecumenical current which is so evident today. This could add great power to the spiritual awakening now taking place.

Despite its weaknesses, the local Church stands for the highest teachings given to man which, I believe, are firmly rooted in our history. The local nucleus of people who profess themselves Christians and join together in fellowship are, therefore, a very important section of any community. Whilst admitting their individual imperfections, they accept the Christian standard as an ideal to which they and their children can aim by maintaining self-disciplined action at a spiritual level. They are a caring section of the community. In these days, missionary work is enlightened and many people overseas are receiving practical help in agriculture, education and industry. Over 90% of all Christian missionary work overseas has been carried out by members of the British Commonwealth and the U.S.A. As this nucleus becomes fused with the extra power available through psychical research, the promise contained in St. Paul's reference to Isaiah in I Cor. 2:9 may well come true — "It is written, eye hath not see, nor ear heard, neither have entered into the heart of man, the things which God hath prepared for them that love him".

The introduction of Synodical Government into the Anglican Church can also open channels through which the Holy Spirit can work. It gives members of the laity great opportunities as they can now participate in the government of the Church.

The writing of this book is in harmony with the general pattern of my life during the past thirty years. There has been a constant reaching out for truth and a constant sharing with others. This pattern has given me many thrills and the rate of meeting those who are ready to respond seems to be accelerating. As these events indicate to me some of the ways in which the power of God is working today, I expect them to continue. I feel a great sense of privilege and a growing sense of purpose in life.